Books by Edmund Keeley

Fiction

THE LIBATION

THE GOLD-HATTED LOVER

THE IMPOSTOR

VOYAGE TO A DARK ISLAND

A WILDERNESS CALLED PEACE

Poetry in Translation

SIX POETS OF MODERN GREECE *(with Philip Sherrard)*

GEORGE SEFERIS: COLLECTED POEMS, 1924–1955 *(with Philip Sherrard)*

C. P. CAVAFY: PASSIONS AND ANCIENT DAYS *(with George Savidis)*

C. P. CAVAFY: SELECTED POEMS *(with Philip Sherrard)*

ODYSSEUS ELYTIS: THE AXION ESTI *(with George Savidis)*

C. P. CAVAFY: COLLECTED POEMS *(with Philip Sherrard and George Savidis)*

ANGELOS SIKELIANOS: SELECTED POEMS *(with Philip Sherrard)*

RITSOS IN PARENTHESES

THE DARK CRYSTAL/VOICES OF MODERN GREECE *(with Philip Sherrard)*

ODYSSEUS ELYTIS: SELECTED POEMS *(ed. with Philip Sherrard)*

GEORGE SEFERIS: COLLECTED POEMS *(with Philip Sherrard)*

YANNIS RITSOS: EXILE AND RETURN, SELECTED POEMS 1967–1974

Fiction in Translation

VASSILIS VASSILIKOS: THE PLANT, THE WELL, THE ANGEL *(with Mary Keeley)*

Criticism

MODERN GREEK WRITERS *(ed. with Peter Bien)*

CAVAFY'S ALEXANDRIA

MODERN GREEK POETRY: VOICE AND MYTH

Exile and Return
Selected Poems
1967-1974

Translated by

Edmund Keeley

The Ecco Press

New York

Yannis Ritsos

Exile and Return

Selected Poems

1967-1974

First published by The Ecco Press in 1985
18 West 30th Street, New York 10001
Published simultaneously in Canada by
Penguin Books Canada Ltd.
2801 John Street
Markham, Ontario, Canada   L3R   1 B4
Printed in the United States of America
First Edition
Library of Congress Cataloging in Publication Data
Ritsos, Giannes, 1909–
Exile and return.
1. Ritsos, Giannes, 1909–   —Translations,
English. I. Title.
PA5629.I7A24   1985   889'.132   85–10222
ISBN 0–88001–017–7

ACKNOWLEDGMENTS

I want to thank, first of all, Mary Keeley and Karen Van Dyck, both of
whom assisted me substantially in the preparation of this volume by providing
first drafts of a number of the poems that I finally selected for inclusion in
the versions that appear here, for which they are not to be held responsible.
Judith Binder gave me a number of valuable suggestions regarding the notes to
the poems from the volume *Repetitions*. I am also grateful to the Hellenic
Studies Committee and the Research Committee of Princeton University,
the Greek Ministry of Culture, and the Translations Program of the National
Endowment for the Humanities, an independent federal agency, for summer
grants in support of my work on this volume. Versions of some of these
translations appeared in *Antaeus*, *The New York Review of Books*, *The
Ontario Review*, *Milkweed Chronicle*, *Chelsea*, *The American Poetry Review*,
Willow Springs Magazine, *Seneca Review*, *Columbia*, *The Pacific Review*,
Crosscurrents, *Translation*, *Ecco Pocket Poetry*, *Grand Street*, *The
Iowa Review*, *Ironwood*, *The New Republic*, *The New England
Review and Breadloaf Quarterly*, *The Missouri Review*, *Greenhouse
Review Press*, *New Letters*, and *Graham House Review*. Twelve translations
appeared in the limited edition *Return and Other Poems* (Parallel
Editions, University, Alabama).

Contents

Contents

Contents

Contents

FROM
Railing
[1968–1969]

Contents

FROM
Doorman's Desk
[1971]

Contents

F R O M
Sidestreet
[1971–1972]

Contents

Contents

Yannis Ritsos is Greece's most prolific contemporary poet, having published, at last count, some ninety-five volumes of poetry, translations, essays, and dramatic works during his more than fifty-year career as a published writer. He and Odysseus Elytis, the 1979 Nobel laureate, are generally acknowledged by their countrymen to be the most important living poets writing in Greek, and in recent years both have found a substantial audience abroad through translations, in Ritsos's case one that extends widely into Eastern as well as Western Europe.

The poems from the eight volumes represented here are characteristic of those that have shaped a major facet of Ritsos's mature work, short free-verse poems usually of eight to sixteen lines (the somewhat longer poems in *Repetitions* are the principal exception) brought together in collections containing between fifty and one hundred and fifty poems normally written over a period of months rather than years. Each of the volumes is given coherence by the repetition of related images and themes. Each reflects the contemporary landscape and history of Greece while projecting a symbolic, at moments even a visionary, representation of what the poet sees as the modern Greek predicament both at a specific point in time and more generally.

The eight volumes that are the source for this anthology were all written during the 1967–1974 dictatorship in Greece and, along with several other Ritsos collections from the same period, constitute on one level what I take to be the most vivid and acute poetic characterization of the aura that dominated those particular years.

The dictatorship arrived suddenly during the early hours of Friday, April 21, 1967, when tanks under the command of a small group of Greek army officers, mostly at the rank of colonel, moved in to take over strategic points in Athens. A characteristic image of this ominous event is provided by the poet in a poem called "Toward Saturday," from the 1975 volume *The Distant*:*

> *The deep voice was heard in the deeper night.*
> *Then the tanks went by. Then day broke.*
> *Then the voice was heard again, shorter, farther in.*
> *The wall was white. The bread red. The ladder*
> *rested almost vertical against the antique lamppost. The old*
> *   woman*
> *collected the black stones one by one in a paper bag.*

The mode here is typical of Ritsos in this late period: no authorial commentary, no manipulating narrative voice, seemingly just the bare facts, but those facts rendered with nightmarish distortion ("the voice . . . shorter, farther in," "the bread red," "black stones") to evoke the latent horror that has come alive in this setting and that pervades Ritsos's poetic landscape after 1967.

The dictatorship under Colonel George Papadopoulos, former head of the Greek intelligence service, retained power for six years through a policy of mixed terror and largesse. Opponents of

---

*This volume appears in its entirety in *Ritsos in Parentheses*, Princeton, 1979, and is therefore not represented here.

the regime were dealt with ruthlessly: imprisoned, tortured, exiled, dispossessed; some villagers, some civil servants, all entrepreneurs foreign and domestic were given loans and special privileges that brought the country close to bankruptcy. Still, there was a continuing resistance both within the armed services and among intellectuals, especially university students. A naval mutiny in 1972 and a student uprising at the Polytechnion (the technological university) in 1973 were both stifled by violent measures, but the first led to a rigged national election that failed to provide the regime with the democratic mask it had sought and the second to the replacement of Papadopoulos by another colonel in the junta, Ioannides, who proved to be even more ruthless and maniacal than his predecessor yet finally no less doomed. The dictatorship came to a sudden end a year later, during the summer of 1974, after a Ioannides plot to overthrow Archbishop Makarios of Cyprus stimulated the Turkish invasion of that island and enough governmental chaos in Athens to occasion the return of democracy under Constantine Karamanlis.

Ritsos's personal experience under the dictatorship is an essential source for themes and images in these volumes. The poet, as a long-standing Communist who had been incarcerated for four years at the end of the civil war in the late forties, was arrested with many others immediately after the April 1967 coup and was shipped to a prison camp on the island of Yiaros, then to another camp on the island of Leros. In 1968, after a month of hospitalization in Athens, he was sent into exile on the island of Samos, under house arrest at his wife's home there, and was finally allowed to return to his Athens apartment in the Agios Nicholaos-Acharnon district in 1970. Even during the less turbulent years that followed the restoration of democracy under Karamanlis, Ritsos lived largely in seclusion, almost in self-exile, his living-room study a kind of cell crammed with paintings and stacked portraits of himself, domestic and foreign editions of his work piled on the floor, and in every corner, stones from the period of his incarceration and after, decorated with his half-erotic, half-idealized drawings of naked men and women taking their shapes from the natural stone contours that he chose to highlight. In the years immediately following the dictatorship Ritsos would receive visitors only briefly after ten in the evening. But in recent years he has gradually emerged from his version of self-exile to become the accessible, public figure who sometimes travels abroad and who often appears at celebrations in honor of one dignitary or another and at cultural occasions sponsored by the Party that has taken him for its laureate.

The context of the poems in this anthology is rarely overtly political (unlike some of Ritsos's early and even recent propagandistic verse), but one level of meaning is clearly intended to reside in the particular historical climate—the imposed mood of the times, if you will—that the dictatorship engendered. One constantly encounters imagery of dislocation, of intimidation, of lethargic and directionless motion, of exile in strange places and even within the confines of a familiar neighborhood, as though the land were under siege and the people in it dispossessed of their normal habitations, their normal means of sustenance both physical and spiritual, or have become so disoriented by circumstances beyond their control that they have lost their power to function as sentient human beings. In several poems the setting is evidently a guarded camp or barracks or building under surveillance, the people living there threatened by mysterious masked figures, thrust into rooms with the dead or the dying for companionship. But more often the poet depicts a recognizable Greek landscape—stones everywhere, olive trees, vineyards, thorny plots and parched fields, whitewashed country houses and monotonous city apartment buildings—only to reveal that this landscape is now subject to violent distortion and the intrusion of unexpected anomalies. The inhabitants, haunted by death, are sometimes seen to be not merely terrorized but petrified, turned into statues, and the statues into animated human beings moving cautiously through abandoned city streets emptied by undefined forces of evil or through a desiccated countryside that carries remembrances of a life that was once at least sufficient but that now seems beyond even ritual rejuvenation, as we see in "Our Land," from the 1967–1968 section of *The Wall Inside the Mirror*:

> *We climbed the hill to look over our land:*
> *fields poor and few, stones, olive trees.*
> *Vineyards head toward the sea. Beside the plow*
> *a small fire smoulders. We shaped the old man's clothes*

into a scarecrow against the ravens. Our days
are making their way toward a little bread and great sunshine.
Under the poplars a straw hat beams.
The rooster on the fence. The cow in yellow.
How did we manage to put our house and our life in order
with a hand made of stone? Up on the lintel
there's soot from the Easter candles year after year:
tiny black crosses marked there by the dead
returning from the Resurrection Service. This land is much
    loved
with patience and dignity. Every night, out of the dry well,
the statues emerge cautiously and climb the trees.

The mutilation of the living in Ritsos's nightmarish landscape
—cripples of one kind or another abound, along with the aged, the
mute, and the blind—is paralleled by the mutilation or destruction
of the Greek tradition and its spiritual resources, both the pagan
and the Christian phases of it. It is here that the poet's vision
transcends the immediate historical climate and suggests deeper
roots for the modern Greek predicament. This world becomes
an emblem of the world beyond; in some poems the current his-
torical reality is made to serve as a metaphor for the death of
gods, heroes, and the faith they are supposed to sustain. At
moments pagan myth and Christian symbolism both seem to
become implicated in the disintegration of contemporary stability
along with the threatening political despotism. The Greek tradi-

tion apparently has to be unmasked for its contributions to spiritual exile side by side with Ritsos's contemporary masked conspirators who bring news of an unwanted trip to the islands.

The 1968–1969 volume called *Repetitions* offers a number of ironic readings of the old mythology, sometimes turning over familiar myths to show a darker, less than heroic underside in the manner of Cavafy: Penelope facing the miserable white-bearded beggar soaked in blood who is her returning husband and collapsing voiceless into a chair to study the slaughtered suitors on the floor "as though seeing her own desires dead there." But we find less overt manifestations of this revisionist sensibility, and the image of a dislocated tradition that it projects, throughout the poems of this period. In one poem a door opens to reveal three hunters burning "the wooden horse" in the oven—all except its eyes, which won't burn. And other poems offer us a Christ figure —"the most innocent liar in the world"—with hands bound or speech entirely mute or a smile covered by cement. The reigning deity in this largely demythologized landscape appears to be an indifferent, unapproachable, infinitely distant ambiguity.

There are few emblems of hope in these volumes from the period of the dictatorship, but there is frequent relief from bleakness in Ritsos's wry sense of humor, especially when we see one of his dislocated and harassed characters managing to make a virtue out of whatever it is that has been placed in his path to torment him, as in "The Unhinged Shutter" from the 1968–1969 volume *Railing*:

> *I told the carpenters, told the builders, told the electricians,*
> *I told the grocer's delivery boy: "Secure that shutter;*
> *all night long, loose-jointed, it bangs in the wind,*
> *won't let me sleep. The owner is away. The house is becoming*
>   *a ruin.*
> *Nobody has been in it for twelve years. Secure it. I'll pay for*
>   *it."*
> *"We don't have the right," they said. "We can't interfere,"*
>   *they said.*
> *"The owner's away. It's a stranger's house." That was just*
>   *what I was hoping for,*
> *what I wanted them to say, to recognize they had no right.*
> *Let the shutter alone, let it bang in the wind over the garden,*
> *over the empty cisterns with the slugs and the lizards,*
> *with the scorpions, the empty spools, the broken glass. That*
>   *noise*
> *gives me an argument, allows me to sleep nights.*

Here and there we also find a glimmer of hope in gestures that suggest a possible change in the course history has taken, though the gestures have a quality of desperation in them, as in the poem "Return," which seems to commemorate the poet's emergence from the detention camp at Partheni, Leros, in 1968 (the original is so situated and dated and serves to mark the division between the two sections of *The Wall Inside the Mirror*, separated by three years). In this poem we see the city first cleared of statues, then of nature and people, left finally to its own desolate devices. Then one man returns to plant his key in the ground "as though entrusting it to an underground hand / or as though planting a tree," and as a result of that gesture, the statues cautiously return as well. And in "Nor This" from the 1972 volume *Muted Poems,* there is a suggestion that the one recourse left for Ritsos's dispossessed and alienated inhabitants is some sort of artistic or symbolic representation of the life that has been lost, and this patiently carved on "a bared kernel of rice." It is a representation that hardly has more sustenance in it than the artifact that bears it, an apparently futile if still heroic gesture of nostalgic recovery and demented resistance: the carving consists of

> *a multitude of war scenes, heroes, dead men, trees, flags,*
> *and that beautiful, crazy deserter who, naked in front of the*
> *   gun barrels,*
> *endlessly drums away on his empty canteen.*

As I have suggested elsewhere,* the starkness of Ritsos's late vision in his shorter poems, with its arid landscape and crippled inhabitants, is usually matched by an aesthetic absoluteness that consists of an uncomplicated syntax and a purified style that leaves little room for figures of speech, little coloring other than

---

*In the essay on Ritsos in *Modern Greek Poetry: Voice and Myth,* Princeton, 1983.

basic adjectives, few images that have not been drained of overt sentiment. The stylistic catharsis of Ritsos's late work serves to provide us with a sense of reality that transcends the merely representational, that reveals both the way things are and a truth below the surface of things.

In these eight volumes from the period of the dictatorship—and in several others not represented here because they have already been amply translated into English*—the revealed reality is often that of an oppressed country haunted by images of horror under skies ruled by what the poet sometimes designates as "the familiar unknown." These are images that not only inhabit the unconscious mind but that can be said to symbolize the consciously felt experiences so many have known in this harsh century. In the poems offered here Ritsos thus speaks not only for those who lived with the aura of Greece's darkest days since World War II and the civil war that followed it, but for all those who have been exiled physically or metaphysically in recent years and who are still struggling to find the return home.

—*Edmund Keeley*

---

*I have in mind especially the translations of Nikos Stangos in *Gestures and Other Poems 1968–70*, London, 1971; of Nikos Germanacos in *Corridor and Stairs*, Ireland, 1976; and of Kimon Friar, and Kostas Myrsiades in *Scripture of the Blind*, Columbus, Ohio, 1979. With a few essential exceptions, I have not included in my selection poems that are available in English elsewhere.

FROM

The Wall Inside

the Mirror

$[1967\text{-}1968, 1971]$

3 / Privilege

This up and down, he says, I don't understand it.
To forget myself I look into the small mirror;
I see the motionless window, I see the wall—
nothing changes inside or outside the mirror.
I let a flower lie on the chair (for as long as it lasts).
I live here, at this number, on this street.
And suddenly they raise me (the chair and the flower too),
they lower me, raise me—I don't know. Luckily
I managed to put this mirror in my pocket.

4 / Elation

The way things have gone empty little by little,
there's nothing left for him to do. He sits alone,
looks at his hands, his fingernails—they're foreign—
he touches his chin again and again, notices
another chin, so simply foreign,
so deeply and naturally foreign that even he himself
begins to take pleasure in its novelty.

5 / Enlightenment

We couldn't stand what was empty, uninhabited. Often we would
    move
the huge mirror to the river bank, a chair
into a tree, and at other times, conversely,
a huge tree into the dining room. Then we would hear
the gunfire behind the sheepfold, late, at dusk,
and though known and expected, it would always startle us—
this our confirmation for the proper placing of words.

6 / Transgression

He opened the door, stood there, looked inside: darkness.
Huge cooking pans hanging on the walls. And suddenly, at the far
    end,
he spotted the glow and the three hunters: they were burning
the wooden horse in the oven—it seemed upright in the oven's red
    mouth
(but its eyes were glass; they wouldn't burn).
He closed the door without a sound. He went out into the garden.

7 / Untitled Events

Memory didn't meet things. Events
were left without room, they dissolved. Of course you could
imagine an ashtray somewhere else, a clothes hanger,
the odor of cologne from some neighborhood barbershop
a little before the stores close Saturday evening—
even the lovely woman who dallied to scratch a tangerine
vanished late at night in the station's glare, smelling her fingers—
distant, distant, exiled, not even adjusting
to the chaotic ammunition chamber with its nylon curtains.

The statues, he said, they too die if you don't look after them.
I've often seen them fallen down, with eyes half-closed. They're
    waiting
too see if anybody notices them, then they get up again. Maybe
    that's why
the stores on the main streets or the small-change shops in the
    suburbs
are full of mirrors both inside and outside:
small, large, all kinds of mirrors. Hung on the walls,
they shine dully—as though indifferent—in secret expectation. They
    mirror
each other in seclusion or sometimes a bit of the street:
the bakery smokestack, a medlar tree, two women,
the wheelbarrow from the small flower shop with its empty clay
    pots.

Late in the evening, around eight, when the stores close, the
    mirrors
empty all at once. Everyone—clerk or owner or customer—
takes a mirror and shuts himself up in his room,
while in the streets outside the stillness of insomnia already begins
    to jell.

9 / Fragmented

That's the way it was: under the flags nobody had a thought.
Later, by the time they'd gathered up the flags and locked them in
   a trunk,
they'd lost all continuity—a leg cut off, a hand,
the head sometimes. In the kitchen the alarm clock rang in
   isolation;
the water boiled, overflowed the pot. They brought in the one who
   was wounded
secretly through the corridor, covered by a blanket from head to
   foot.
Then, suddenly, we heard the howl in the farthest room.
Everyone covered his mouth with a hand as though he'd been the
   one who'd cried out.

Well past midnight the bugle sounded. Nobody
knew what was up. They all looked out from behind their windows.
Lights turned off, curtains drawn. Only the man in charge of water
went outside, climbed the stairs, came down. His dog
began to bay at the moon. The five masked men
entered the communal bathroom, throwing their clothes over the
    divider
piece by piece: pants, undershirts, shorts, shoes,
five wristwatches. They didn't throw their masks.

He went out, late at night, with the wild resolution
not to go anywhere, not to speak to anyone. The lights
had come on in the small clinic. Violent wind
was breaking branches. The trees were on the run. And he, like a
  rider
astride the jet black horse of night, self-sufficient,
felt the flaps of his overcoat beating his knees
like the wings of a huge door forced open.

We climbed the hill to look over our land:
fields poor and few, stones, olive trees.
Vineyards head toward the sea. Beside the plow
a small fire smoulders. We shaped the old man's clothes
into a scarecrow against the ravens. Our days
are making their way toward a little bread and great sunshine.
Under the poplars a straw hat beams.
The rooster on the fence. The cow in yellow.
How did we manage to put our house and our life in order
with a hand made of stone? Up on the lintel
there's soot from the Easter candles, year by year:
tiny black crosses marked there by the dead
returning from the Resurrection Service. This land is much loved
with patience and dignity. Every night, out of the dry well,
the statues emerge cautiously and climb the trees.

13 / After Rain

After the rain there were those birds and small clouds.
The sunset came quietly, with a lot of color. A kind of pink
trembled on the water, side by side with orange. Strange, he said,
that there are colors, that we see. In the canteen they sell
Christmas cards, chocolates, cigarettes.
The secret is for you to forget. They turn on the lights. The sick
are in harmony with the dusk. Under the trees, two benches
and the long table for the guards. You know, he said,
there's a peculiar kind of fish that doesn't speak.

We waited month after month. We watched the road. Nothing.
No messenger appeared. The path all stones and thorns.
October, November, December. And the long table
forgotten under the trees. Until finally
the supervisor arrived, set the twelve glasses
on the table. One of them fell to the ground;
it broke into smithereens. So we'd have to start waiting from the
     beginning again.

15 / Startled

They'd left a slice of bread on the stone.
The bird stood there; he pecked at it. The crone came back:
"I didn't leave that for you," she told the bird. She took the bread,
crumbled it up finely, scattered the crumbs for the bird.
The bird looked at her square in the eyes; he didn't eat.

Half a glass of water on the table. All around him,
gathered up silently, melancholy things:
a letter opener, comb, matches, a cigarette
smoking itself in the ash tray,
and in the courtyard outside a strong wind
ruffling the down of the wild ducks shot dead.

She changed the water in the vase. She threw the wilted daisies
into the garbage pail, arranged others in their place.
That familiar sadness over something left out or postponed
clung to her fingers. Through the window opposite
the old man drew up a basket held by a string.
In the basket there was an old doll without any arms.

They sang with their mouths wide open—
it seemed the voice emerged directly from the tongue's root,
without precaution, pretense, manipulation. That's why
they were all so beautiful, with large, eager hands,
private feet, audacious hair. And he:
"If I could only have their voice," he said to himself, "or at least
their tongue in my closed mouth"—and with the word "closed"
he again sensed his particular fate. He lowered his eyelids,
then went into the other room, lay down and slept. In his sleep
he still heard the grinding wheel sharpening the huge knives.

19 / Young Girl Sulking

To think that she couldn't be something else—anything else.
     Opposite her
that invisible mirror, looking at itself, seeing
her motion before she moved. And outside, in the garden,
her girl friends calling to her, skipping rope,
swinging under the trees, covering their breasts,
armpits, hair, with lemon blossoms. She, as though not hearing,
stitched away with the giant, archaic sewing machine, in the room,
stitched hard, almost violently: cold white sheets for a bridal bed.
And opposite, the mirror showed her over and over again that she
     was beautiful.

When he went upstairs, he didn't find anyone. He came down
     again,
went through the rooms one by one, searched: nothing.
As he was leaving he heard the squeaking sound, in the garden,
beside the fountain. The wooden horse
was opening its left flank. The twelve wounded swordsmen
carefully climbed down the small ladder, went inside the house. He
managed to lock them in, vaulted inside the horse, secured the
     latch-door,
lit his cigarette. As he puffed away like that, safe and sound,
the smoke came out of the horse's eyes. The sun went down,
and he, still inside, explored the impression he made from the
     outside.

The same footsteps ahead, the same behind. The wall
the same on both sides. The lizard sits in its hole,
the spider on the ceiling. If it begins to rain
where will the bird go, and the man
with his old hat, his dirty handkerchief in his pocket,
his two grains of salt on the broken roof tile?

He half-opened the door, looked in: nobody there. The hall empty.
    A huge
black, bare table; around it tall black chairs with upright backs.
He hid behind the black curtain. Soon
the delegates entered quietly, took their places. A bell
sounded suddenly. The messenger came in, raised his hand,
opened his mouth wide—no voice emerged. The delegates,
again without a sound, hid under the table. Then
the naked dancing girl rushed in, jumped up on the table, danced,
    left—
a flower from her hair fell to the floor. He,
reaching from behind the curtain, just managed to grab it
as the trap door opened, swallowing the delegates,
the table and chairs, the chandelier, the president's bell.

23 / Wax Images

He entered the showroom. The lighting was dim. He studied
the wax images: naked, nicely colored; he liked them—
stimulating, almost erotic. Exquisite bodies, as though each
had been shaped by the same prototype, at various ages. When he
      raised his eyes,
he recognized his face in theirs. At that moment
he heard footsteps in the corridor. He undressed quickly, stood
      there motionless.
They came in, circled the showroom, stopped finally in front of
      him. "This one
seems less natural," the woman said, and she pointed him out.
He heard his eyelids lowering; they closed.

Poor soil, very poor; burnt shrubs, stones—
we loved these stones, we worked them. Time goes by.
Brilliant sunsets. A mauve glow on the windows.
Behind the windows earthen pots, unmarried girls.
Mists come up from the olive grove. When evening falls,
the procession of those wearing veils starts up from the cypress
    trees;
their gait, somehow rigid, has a sad, archaic dignity;
you can tell suddenly from the gait that their knees
are marble, broken, stuck back together with cement.

In those days everything was strange. The monks
left the monasteries, some turned into peddlers,
others sold wild berries. They hid their robes
in a basket or in a black button-lined kerchief. With dusk,
they wore their robes again. They climbed the trees,
caught owls, plucked them, then cooked them
behind the cemetery walls. From a point opposite
they watched the fires reflected on the shore. The next day
the monks again sold wild berries, spools of yarn, pocket combs,
and the shore was covered into the distance with down feathers
    and bones.

In front of the door they read a list. Those
who heard their names got ready in a hurry—
a torn suitcase, a bundle, the rest left behind.
The place emptied steadily, shrank. Those who remained gathered
    in tightly.
With a certain reticence and solemnity they set up a forgotten
    alarm clock
in the far corner of the room. From then on, every night,
each taking his turn, they wound it, waiting serenely for it to go off
at 6:15 the next morning so that they could go out and wash. One
    day
it went off at midnight. They got up, washed—the moon was out—
then sat around the alarm clock to smoke a cigarette.

27 / Return

The statues left first. A little later
the trees, people, animals. The land
became entirely desert. The wind blew.
Newspapers and thorns circled in the streets.
At dusk the lights went on by themselves.
A man came back alone, looked around him,
took out his key, stuck it in the ground
as though entrusting it to an underground hand
or as though planting a tree. Then he climbed
the marble stairs and gazed down at the city.
Cautiously, one by one, the statues returned.

November 1967–January 1968
Concentration Camp for Political Detainees
Partheni, Leros

The hill with olive trees. A little higher up
another hill with olive trees. The river is flowing
down in the ravine—you can't hear it. Poor women,
outside the graveyard walls, sell wild flowers
tied up with faded thread unraveled
from the undershirt of the forgotten soldier.

Then the sun sets. The olive trees darken
deeply, so deeply, for no reason at all,
just like the stone angel and the bronze rider.

A morning of islands and marble lions,
this land that bleeds and hurts you,
with yellow thorns all the way to the customs house,
when the ram comes down the hillside
with flared nostrils, a flower between his teeth,
and the stones behind him roll toward the sea, there
where the beautiful deserters are swimming naked,
looking into the distance, in front of them, into the white water,
looking at the red line left by the wounded dolphin.

The dead nailed to the walls, next to the ads
for the national loan, the dead set up on the sidewalks,
in wooden stands put up for public officials, with flags, helmets,
cardboard masks.
                        The dead
no longer have any place to hide, they don't control
their dry bones (merchandised deaths, crates
raised by winches, yellow paper full of pins). The dead
are increasingly in danger.
                                And he, with foresight, carrying an
            umbrella,
walking high up, on the electric cables, rope-walker,
above the parade, with his eyes bound by a handkerchief,
while the first drops of rain appeared.
                                Then the cloudburst.
The bugles called the women to wring out the flags.
They'd locked themselves in their basements and eaten their keys.

Naked like this, unarmed, surrounded by so much noise,
he heard silence rising inside him. On the wall
he saw a spider climbing slowly, calmly,
magnified, projected far into empty space,
with its crooked legs, its fat head. He remembered then
a boat loaded with cotton. The owner, naked,
had given up his oars and, motionless, climbed
a huge moving cloud, aware maybe
that from somewhere he was being watched. A secret satisfaction
glowed in his features and his body, which, yesterday evening,
entirely by chance, he had washed and manicured.

The grasping branches, the drum of night,
the echoes in hidden recesses, the great river
dividing the nonexistent landscape in fantasy;
and the second drum, louder than the first,
and the trembling in the hand that knocked, waiting
for the answer from behind the door, from inside,
when there wasn't a door, nor an inside, nor an outside,
only the marble trough and the dry well
and the slavishness of this waiting: spelling out
the pace of a horse without a rider
in the light of a supposedly green bolt of lightning
down in low hills, laid waste
by the unknown and its frequent repetition
in chimneys, prisons, statues, trees.

33 / Sunday Excursion

The good olive trees, the sea—a sense of duration.
Petros would like to pray. Yannis
stands alone beyond the light, concentrating. The frog
moves cautiously, stops, eavesdrops.
So they have their meaning, the weighed oranges
beside the dirt road, inside plastic bags
that hold one or two kilos. And the noble islands
have their meaning, traveling along the far horizon,
and the white cloud with the wound in its side—
white from opposition or its spilled blood.

He sets the chairs in the air. He sets the people
on the chairs. With his hands he pushes
the wooden legs. They move back and forth. A lightness,
rhythm, successful swaying, the inexhaustible,
like those swings back then, on the tall trees, beside the house
where the consumptive women died peacefully
listening to the squeaking of the bronze rings
in the gardens of Kifissia with their gentle dampness—
time passing, the back and forth of an afternoon,
as though back and forth existed.

The dice, the sewing machine, the folding measure,
the compass, the bicycle, the microscope,
the penknife, the quivering eyelid, time,
the forester's boots, the clock on the wall,
the mouth that calls without a voice, without teeth,
the horse turning the millstone, the horse in bed, the carnival horse
cut out of cardboard with its fringe of green—
from a hole in its side emerges the dead man's
pale hand barely holding a flower.

The hall had three large doors, all wide open.
The guests entered wearing long, precious vestments,
with uniform white bandages on their foreheads.
The host wasn't at all visible, seated
under his carved, gilded canopy. Then
the coal miner came in with his lamp, barefoot,
leaving on the marble slabs the imprint
of his broad soles—black from coal dust—
which grew in size behind him like full-scale bodies.
Outside the night with its distorting mirrors
and the demonstrators with their oil lamps and iron rods
burning the newspapers at the foot of the stairway,
along with the carts and the crutches of the disabled,
while the sky was left alone in its black light,
free up there, high up, above the conflagration.

37 / In the Depths

He saw the diver stir deep down in the water
with soft, carnal movements. Beyond
he saw the clay penis and the statue's feet
stepping firmly on the sea floor. And he also saw
the clay woman spread out, waiting,
one knee slightly raised, with a red,
totally red fish on her belly. Except
that the seaweed didn't move, there was no seaweed,
and the coin they threw in from above descended slowly
until it stopped a hand's width from the woman's mouth.

He didn't hear them at all as they came up the stairs.
He didn't have time to think about where they may have found
    the key.
That which he called duration was cut—and he didn't even see
the incision on the floor. They drew
the huge black curtain in front of him, while above him
he could hear the scraping sound of the nickel rings—
high up, on the invisible wire, loosely stretched,
high up, in the clandestine sky that finally belonged to him.

Hallway, door, hallway, door; half-light;
afternoon leaning toward dusk. All the doors
open to the far end. People made of plaster, bent over,
are sitting alone, each to a bench. The last,
in the innermost hallway, barely distinguishable
like the head of a pin:
                    "Distance," he was saying, "neutralizes
volume, maybe pain as well." That's what he was saying.
Nobody believed him or even paid attention to him. On the right,
through the dust-covered, barred window,
you could see, passing by under artificial neon sunshine,
a tall, immense bus full of people on an excursion,
plaster boys, plaster girls with spearguns,
with those long plastic flippers,
very blue or yellow, hanging in the windows.

(Was the absence of a conclusion, then, the essence?)

We crossed under the arcades of the dead. As we came out,
the glare from the whitewashed wall struck our eyes
as an open hand against the chest. We stood there.
For a moment we closed our eyes, inhaling deeply
the smell of burnt besom.
                              "O that
ungraspable and unrepentant thing," the foreign woman said—
and maybe by that she meant our frequent disobedience to death,
while the cicadas cooled their bellies on the marble ruins
in that pure gold noontime, and a slender thread of water
from the mountain's spring snow came down, binding
the right rear hoof of the great stone bull.

People, years, things: abandoned, dislocated,
at some point jelled into a grimace; and their shadow motionless
on the stripped floor. A silly woman
moves among them bending down and bending down again
as though bowing to the unforeseen, as though excusing herself,
gathering one by one, with inexplicable pleasure, the beads
from her broken necklace. Every now and then she stands up
    straight,
counts, recollects, compares—things she never bothered to figure
    out
when the necklace was around her neck. But now she realizes
that the largest bead is missing, the middle one. And she no longer
    searches
because within some deeper verification she discovered suddenly
that which was always missing in her, that which is always missing:
this lightness, like this piece of broken string
that hangs quietly from her fingers and that she now studies.

Night fell suddenly. The land turned dark.
Only the four benches along the deserted square
shone secretly from the dew. A woman
strolled under the trees, her eyes shut.
Behind her came the two bicycles with lights out.
All had reached an advance agreement with death:
the chair's shadow, the spider, the poem,
the violin case open on the bed. Of course
this agreement too was a new postponement
to gain time, to think, to observe
the four benches and the great curtain drawing closed.

He searched constantly, without reason or need.
In the ashes he found small uninhabited islands
with their old churches full of wind.
Outside one church there was a chair.
Below, on the rocks, huge sea urchins
shaded by an unmoving cloud. After that
he had nothing to add. Clearly he went out of his way
to avoid saying the word d e a t h.

They came by here too. They went away. Black stones,
broken trees, broken traffic lights. In the street
broken windows, tacks, boxes, string.
Inside the empty room the great table was set,
on every plate a severed head. In the doorway
the headless dancer.

                "Lord," he said, "I'll run,
catch up with them, Lord. I'll run."

                        Down at the river
they were washing the baskets from the grape harvest.
The cicadas went wild.

The cloud passed over. The moon appeared frozen.
You could see the marble stairway and the chair,
then the bare tree with its cluster of bats.
The stage director had hung the bats there.
In the doorway stood the madman. He put down
a package made of oiled newspaper.
"It's bones," he said. "For the dog."
The dog had died years ago. The others
turned to face the wall, covered themselves from head to foot
with the old stolen army blankets.

With the coming of autumn, chimneys are inscribed more
    accurately on the sunset.
The lame seamstress climbs down the stairs cautiously.
"You'll fall," the cook yells at her from above.
The toilet is as narrow as a child's tomb.
When night comes, the poorest dogs in the world gather together
and squat outside on the church steps. Then
everyone waits to fathom the wind's words.
The dead wait to be born again.

The wall drips moisture. The windows are shut.
Not even wheel tracks in the dry mud. The clouds
come down the hills, as low as the plain. The wind is blowing.
Along the whole length of the passageway embalmed frogs
stand rigid on their hind legs. Now
we'll have to complete their jumping
without knowing the "how" of it and the "why." Above us,
on a yellow rope stretched between one wall and the other,
hang the keys to our missing cloth suitcases.

Empty churches on the hills. Down on the plain
the cattle, houses, vineyards. The sky motionless
between changing clouds. The black stain
motionless on the wall—blacker in the mirror.
He scratches at the stain with his fingernails; the nails fray.
Then he gets paint, covers the wall in gold. As though by mistake
he gives his nose a stroke of paint, then his cheeks. Golden like that
he looks at himself in the mirror. He laughs, eyes closed:
death's eternal jester (as we call him),
hiding in his pocket the three large, rusted nails.

Athens, Samos
March–October 1971

FROM

Stones

$[1968]$

Later the statues were completely hidden by weeds. We didn't
    know
if the statues had grown smaller or the weeds taller. Only
a huge bronze arm could be seen above the terebinth
shaping an unseemly, terrible benediction. The woodcutters
went by on the lower road—they didn't turn their heads.
The women didn't lie down with their men. Nights
we would hear the apples falling into the river one by one; and
    then
the stars quietly sawing through that raised bronze arm.

May 16, 1968

Calm sea with barely perceptible cracks in it; feigned light
coating the low overcast. Don't remember,
don't forget. The present, he says. What present? At night
mute messengers arrived, sat down on the stone steps,
took out their handkerchiefs, spread them on their knees,
folded their handkerchiefs again. They left. One of them
had a scar stretching from his temple down across his cheek. He
    stood there,
pointed toward the sea, tightened the rope around his waist.
Then we put our oil lamps down on the ground and saw our
    shadows—
hairy, huge, boneless—climb the white wall.

May 18, 1968

Why are you taking me this way? Where does this road go? Tell
me.
I can't see a thing. This isn't a road. Just stones.
Black beams. Lamp bracket. At least if I had
that cage—not this bird cage but that other one
with the heavy wire netting, with the naked statues. Back then
when they threw the dead bodies down from the roof terrace, I
didn't say anything,
I gathered up those statues—felt sorry for them. Now I know:
the last thing that dies is the body. So speak to me.
Why are you taking me this way? I can't see a thing. It's great I
can't see.
The biggest obstacle against thinking to the end is glory.

May 19, 1968

The way things have ended up, nobody—so we say—is at fault. One
     left,
another was killed, the rest—how account for it now?
The seasons go about their business as usual. The oleanders
     blossom.
The shade goes all the way around the tree. The motionless jug
stayed in the hot sun, dried out; the water survived. Still, he says,
we could have moved the jug here or there
depending on the time of day and the shade, round and round the
     tree,
circling until we found the rhythm, dancing, forgetting
the jug, the water, the thirst—not thirsting, dancing.

May 20, 1968

Lizards large and small in the wall's crevices. Spiders,
a mass of spiders in the gone summer's baskets. And he
doesn't care any more even about the statues. He didn't become a
    statue.
His hands left to rest on his bare knees. These fingernails,
the hairs, the ring (what ring?), foreign, foreign.
Having nothing to hide, he has nothing to expose.

May 22, 1968

He withdrew from our group little by little, as though somehow
     grieving,
as though somehow strangely calm, as though he'd discovered
something great and incommunicable: a headless statue, a star, a
     truth,
a final and single truth. Which one? we asked him. He
didn't speak, as though he knew we neither could
nor wanted to learn.
                              We, his friends,
threw the first stone. That's just what his adversaries wanted. At
     the trial
they asked him, asked him again. He: not a word. Then the
     president
hit the bell hard, yelled out, raged: quiet in the courtroom,
the silence of the accused is not to be heard. The conviction
     unanimous.
One by one we turned and put our foreheads against the wall.

May 24, 1968

Nothing new, he says. Men are killed or die, but mostly
they grow old, grow old, grow old—the teeth, the hair, the hands,
    the mirrors.
That lamp chimney broke; we patched it up with newspaper.
And the worst of all: whatever you find out has a certain value has
    already gone. Then
a great silence takes over. Summer arrives. The trees
are tall and green—very provocative. The cicadas cry out.
Evenings the mountains turn blue. From up there
dusky people descend. They limp downhill (that is, pretend to
    limp).
They throw their dead dogs into the river, then sad and seemingly
    angry,
they fold up their mats, scratch their balls and gaze at the moon
    on the water. Only that
inexplicable thing about them: playing at being cripples, with
    nobody to watch them—

May 25, 1968

A sudden breeze came up. The heavy shutters creaked.
Leaves rose from the ground. They left, left.
Only the stones remained. We'll have to get along with these
      now—
with these, with these, he repeats. When night comes down
the great black mountain and throws our keys in the well—
my stone, my stone, he says, one by one I will carve
my unknown faces and my body, with one hand
clenched tight, raised above the wall.

May 30, 1968

We were to stay here, who knows how long. Little by little
we lost track of time, of distinctions—months, weeks,
days, hours. It was fine that way. Below, way down,
there were oleanders; higher up, the cypress trees; above that,
    stones.
Flocks of birds went by; their shadows darkened the earth.
That's the way it happened in my day too, the old man said. The
    iron bars
were there in the windows before they were installed, even if they
    weren't visible. Now,
from seeing them so much, I think they're not there—I don't see
    them.
Do you happen to see them? Then they called the guards. They
    opened the door,
pushed in two handcarts full of watermelons. The old man spoke
    again:
Hell, no matter how much your eyes clear up, you don't see a thing.
You see the big nothing, as they say: whitewash, sun, wind, salt.
You go inside the house: no stool, no bed; you sit on the ground.
Small ants amble through your hair, your clothes, into your mouth.

June 5, 1968

So. This alone? he said. We're to base our pride
on the mistakes of others? What pride? What justice?
And not on our own virtues? Teacher, Teacher, we were well
    acquainted
with your mimicry: justice, freedom—and that celestial
smile of yours (so we called it) when doors opened and the crowds
    ran,
ran behind you shouting, leaving their houses open
to the sun, to the air, to thieves. And when, the next night,
the thirteenth raised his glass, we knew by then:
everything was prearranged. The dead stretched out on their beds,
and under the beds your cardboard shoes—
red, imperial, with tiny mirrors glued all over them.

June 6, 1968

Who was it (and when) who hung this black bell
right above the table, in the middle of the ceiling? Months ago,
    years ago?
Bent over our plates, we hadn't noticed it. We never raised
our heads a little higher—why would we? But now
we know: it's there, unmovable. Who happened to see it first?
    Who mentioned it to us
since no one of us talks? Maybe one night following the path of
    the glass
as we drained the last drop of wine our eye caught a glimpse of it
    through empty clouded glass. Right away
we bent down even farther. Hungry or not, we eat, always waiting
from one minute to the next for a great invisible hand to strike the
    bell
nine or twelve times or once only, infinitely only, insubordinately
    only,
while inside ourselves we're already counting in case we manage at
    least to synchronize with the bell's tolling.

June 14, 1968

From one rented room to another—a suitcase,
a table, an ancient bed, a chair.
The mattress straw, smashed bedbugs, ejaculations.
Nobody has a house of his own—always moving.
Our common fate, he says—soothing thought. That tree too:
motionless, peaceful, blossoming, in a world all its own,
looking at nothing—focused entirely on its flowering,
mirrored in a huge inscrutable glass door.

June 14, 1968

63 / Midnight

Light on her feet, dressed in black, her footsteps couldn't be
    heard at all.
She went through the arcade. The lantern was out. As she climbed
the stone stairs they called out "Halt." Her face
was steaming in the darkness, all white. Under her apron
she was hiding the violin. "Who goes there?" She didn't answer.
She stood there motionless, her hands high, holding the violin
tightly between her knees. She was smiling.

June 15, 1968

Tall eucalyptus with a broad moon.
A star trembles on the water.
The sky white, silver.
Stones, flayed stones all the way up.
Near the shallow water you could hear
a fish jump twice, three times.
Ecstatic, grand orphanhood—freedom.

October 21, 1968
Concentration Camp for Political Detainees
Partheni, Leros

FROM

Repetitions

$[1968\text{-}1969]$

67 / The New Oracle

Two years long we suffered badly from drought—not a green leaf,
not a bird or even a locust in Boeotia. "Consult somebody," they
    advised us,
"consult the Pythia." We looked around, found her, consulted her.
    And she,
"Consult the oracle of Trophonius," she told us. For our part,
we had no idea if and where such an oracle existed. And, worst of
    all,
these days you don't come across a Saon, guided by divine
    enlightenment,
to follow a swarm of bees, to learn and advise us about
the secret law of the unsolvable and the inexplicable, which would
    have eased things a bit.
Everyone was calling for practical guidelines right now. They
    couldn't wait, in too much of a hurry.
Anyway, without doubt we needed a new oracle of Trophonius,
so, out of contributions, with some scurrying around and some
    talk, we rigged one up as best we could.

March 17, 1968

We ought to protect our dead and their power in case someday
our adversaries disinter them and carry them off. Then,
without their protection, our danger would double. How could we
    go on living
without our houses, our furniture, our fields, especially without
the tombs of our ancestral warriors and wise men? Let's not forget
how the Spartans stole the bones of Orestes from Tegea. Our
    enemies
should never know where we've buried our dead. But
how are we ever to know who our enemies are
or when and from where they might show up? So no grand
    monumental graves,
no gaudy decorations—things like that draw attention, stir envy.
    Our dead
have no need of that; satisfied with little, unassuming and silent
    now,
they're indifferent to hydromel, votive offerings, vanities. Better
a plain stone and a pot of geraniums, a secret sign,
or nothing at all. For safety's sake, we might do well to hold them
    inside us if we can,
or better still, not even know where they lie.
The way things have turned out in our time, who knows,
we ourselves might dig them up, throw them out someday.

March 20, 1968

69 / After the Defeat

After the heavy losses that the Athenians suffered at Aegospotami,
     and a little later,
after our final defeat, free talk is dead, so too is the Periclean glory,
the flowering of Art, the Gymnasia and the Symposia of our
     learned men. Now
deep silence and gloom in the Agora, and the Thirty Tyrants
     unaccountable.
Everything, even what is most ours, becomes ours by default,
     without
the possibility of any appeal, any defense or vindication,
any formal protest even. Our papers and books are burned,
our country's honor thrown out in the garbage. And if we might
     ever be allowed
to bring in an old friend as a witness, he would refuse to come
for fear of finding himself in our situation—and rightly so. That's
     why
it's really all right to be here: maybe we can establish a new
     relationship with nature,
gazing out, beyond the barbed wire, at a bit of sea, the stones, the
     grass,
or maybe a cloud at sunset, heavy, violet, touching. And maybe
someday we'll find a new Kimon, secretly guided
by the same eagle, to dig down and uncover the iron point of our
     spear,

rusted, that too eaten away, so that he can carry it officially
   through Athens
in a funeral procession or victory celebration, with music and
   wreaths.

March 21, 1968

She who, that first night, slept with a god, not knowing it
—only because of his heavy worldly odor and his broad hairy chest,
almost the same as her husband's yet so very different, did she
seem to have guessed and sensed something—how was she now to
    sleep
with a mortal? And what did she care about Amphitryon's presents
    or even
her child's twelve labors and his immortality, or for that matter,
    hers? She
reminisces about one night only, waits for one night only again,
    late, the moment
when outside in the garden Ursa dims and near it Orion
shows his silver shoulders (O God, how sweet the roses smell)—
she, ready as she can be, when her husband is away hunting, always
    ready, bathed,
naked, puts on her earrings again, her bracelets, and lingers in
    front of the mirror
combing her long hair, still thick, even if dry and dyed.

March 23, 1968

So, even with a severed tongue, Philomela recounted her
    tribulations,
weaving them one by one into her robe with patience and faith,
with modest colors—violet, ash, white and black—and as is always
    true
with works of art, the black is left over. All the rest—
Procne, Tereus with his axe, their pursuit in Daulis,
even the cutting out of the tongue—we consider insignificant,
    things we forget.
That robe of hers is enough, secret and precise, and her
    transformation
at the crucial moment into a nightingale. Still, we say: without all
    the rest,
those things now contemptible, would this brilliant robe and the
    nightingale exist?

April 9, 1968

Tonight, during talk of how all things age, fade, cheapen—
beautiful women, heroic deeds, poems—we suddenly remembered
the celebrated ship that they brought to Corinth one spring
      evening,
now eaten through, the paint gone, oarlocks removed,
all patches, holes, memories. The great procession through the
      forest,
with torches, wreaths, flutes, athletic games for the young. Truly
      a grand offering
to Poseidon's temple, that aged Argo. The night lovely, and the
      chanting of the priests.
An owl hooted above the temple's pediment, and the dancers
      leaping with light feet
on the ship, their mimicry of crude action with unbecoming charm,
      the movement
of nonexistent oars, the sweat and the blood. Then an old sailor
spat at the ground by his feet, moved off to the grove nearby and
      took a leak.

May 7, 1968

It wasn't that she didn't recognize him in the light from the
      hearth; it wasn't
the beggar's rags, the disguise—no. The signs were clear:
the scar on his knee, the pluck, the cunning in his eye. Frightened,
her back against the wall, she searched for an excuse,
a little time, so she wouldn't have to answer,
give herself away. Was it for him, then, that she'd used up
      twenty years,
twenty years of waiting and dreaming, for this miserable
blood-soaked, white-bearded man? She collapsed voiceless into a
      chair,
studied the slaughtered suitors on the floor as though seeing
her own desires dead there. And she said "Welcome" to him,
hearing her voice sound foreign, distant. In the corner, her loom
covered the ceiling with a trellis of shadows; and all the birds she'd
      woven
with bright red thread in green foliage, now,
this night of the return, suddenly turned ashen and black,
flying low on the level sky of her final enduring.

September 21, 1968

We had our altars, churches, oracles. With our own eyes
we'd seen the golden dove and the woodcutter's axe
fall to the ground. Secret voices—the leaves, the birds, the
    springhead—
told us what to do, what not to do. And we had strong support
from the witches with their cauldrons and their coffee cups. And
    from above
the deep-throated oak. We too had something to consult for
    advice, question
about our sheep, our children, the pomegranate tree, the one-eyed
    cow,
about the donkey, the melon patch, the clay pot. And the answer
    always
(however much it might change every time, each time in the same
    tone)
sure, strong, imperative, irrevocable. We were somehow
    reassured—
others were responsible for the decision that would bring success
    or failure. We
had only to submit and perform, with eyes lowered. Now,
they've turned everything upside down—altars, churches,
    graveyards. The bones
thrown out in the alley. They've even chopped down the sacred
    oak—our counselor.
We no longer have anyone to ask for advice, to confide in. Arkes

circulates in the marketplace with his bloodied axe belted to his
    waist,
and not even a golden down feather from the dead oracular dove
to flutter in the kitchen skylight or on the dusty oleanders;
only the water of denial drips late at night in the empty stable,
and it is peaceful, with an insidious peacefulness like the first, like
    the last.

October 6, 1968

With the gods overthrown like that, nobody knew which way to
    turn.
The sick stayed in bed with their eyes closed.
Their woolen socks rotted away in their shoes, along with two
    flowers in a glass.
The cunning ones adjusted quickly. They put on their good
    clothes again,
circulated in the marketplace, discussed things, did business. They
    undertook
the defense against the incursion. They changed the names of
    streets
and temples: improvised substitutions. Zeus and Dione
gave way to Jesus and the Virgin. Theodosius
added the finishing touches—what altars and sanctuaries, and that
    huge tree
overwhelmed by votive offerings.
                              And still
a number of people (including the best) haven't yet come to their
    senses. They're waiting once again
for better gods and people. They fume, protest,
dream, hope. We, the few (who, to some degree anyway, think a
    little),
we've given up such luxuries, given up thinking itself.
We plow our small plot of land, look at the clouds once in a while,
calm now, almost secure. One day we found, thrown into a ditch,
that statuette that used to strike metal tools with its wand

and give out prophetic sounds. For a moment that moved us. We
    said
we'd set it aside for safekeeping somewhere. But what's the point?
    Are we supposed to cling to relics these days?
And what if they turned it up on us? We left it there. Covered it
    with two handfuls of dirt.
The dog was in a hurry. It smelled the trees. Large raindrops were
    already falling.

October 7, 1968

Everything was decreed, safeguarded, worked out logically,
you might even say humanely. The municipal churches played
    their part as well.
Athena watched over justice; always present herself, if invisible,
to preside over the meetings of the Areopagus. And if the voting
split exactly in half, then the scales of justice
tilted toward the defendant.
                           Those were good days—
they don't seem real now. Did they or didn't they exist? Maybe
we simply dreamed them up. Maybe frequent recollection
changed them into rainy autumn sunsets.
                           When we would celebrate
    the plowing,
as the priest bent over to dig the first furrow at the foot of the
    Acropolis
he would recite beautiful words: "Never refuse fire and water to
    anyone.
Never point out the wrong road to anyone who asks. Never let a
    body
go unburied. Do not kill the bull that draws the plow."

Beautiful words, truly—but only words. In practice, then and now,
fire is for the neighbor's crops and water is for the floods,
and the bull with the red ribbons is bubbling away in the thief's
    cauldron.

Only the plow, all alone (maybe steered by an invisible hand),
still plows the barren field full of mallow and wild lilies.

October 18, 1968

It wasn't by chance that Marpessa preferred Idas over Apollo,
despite her passion for the god, despite his incomparable beauty—
the kind that made myrtle tremble into blossom as he went by. She
never dared raise her eyes above his knees.
Between his toenails and his knees, what an inexhaustible world,
what exquisite journeys and discoveries between his toenails and
    his knees. Still,
at the ultimate moment of choice, Marpessa lost her nerve: What
    would she do
with a bequest as grand as that? A mortal, she would grow old one
    day.
She suddenly imagined her comb with a tuft of white hair in it
left on a chair beside the bed where the immortal one would rest
    shimmering,
she thought also of time's fingerprints on her thighs, her fallen
    breasts
in front of the black metal mirror. Oh no—and she sank as though
    dead
against Idas' mortal shoulder. And he lifted her up in his arms
    like a flag
and turned his back on Apollo. But as he left, almost arrogantly,
one could hear something like the sound of cloth ripping (a
    strange sound):
a corner of the flag was held back, trapped by the god's foot.

October 28, 1968

No, it isn't that Apollo reneged on his promise
and took the conviction out of Cassandra's words by spitting in
    her face
to nullify the gift he'd granted her, thereby making her prophecies
useless both for her and for others—no. It's just that
nobody wants to believe the truth. And when you see
the net in your bath, you think they've gotten it out
for your fishing trip tomorrow, and neither inside you
nor outside do you hear, on the palace's marble stairs,
the dark intimation coming up with hapless Cassandra's wailing.

June 7, 1969

Not even the gods can stand solitude. When Apollo
returned to Aliartos after slaying the Python and by himself
built his own altar in the sacred wood, beside the fountain of
    Telephusa,
he looked all around him: not a soul. Lord of the land,
oh yes, but alone—so he reflected. Who will run the place?
Who will enjoy its mysterious sayings? And, above all,
who will admire his rich head of hair falling over his shoulders?

So he obliged the first ship passing by on its way to Pylos
to run aground near Chrissa and sink in the sandy depths there,
and he held, as guards for his temple and its prophets, those
who had sailed from heavily wooded Knossos to sell
tobacco and oil—even if they were just small-time merchants,
    ignorant young men
and simple rowers.
                That's how it happened. And they decorated
Apollo's first temple, interpreted every which way
his great oracles. That statue of him, in the museum,
shows him with a double-minded smile hovering between bliss and
    tolerance.

June 8, 1969

Maybe because they indicated distances and served to rest travelers,
maybe for other reasons forgotten over the years,
the Greeks nurtured a real devotion to the Herms,
especially the credulous working class and even more so the young
men and the girls:
                    during their evening strolls in the summer
they would stand for hours in the street to look at them. They
        offered them
fruit, sweet delicacies and small animals (birds or rabbits),
crowned their well-groomed heads with boughs
and beautifully twined flowers—because they, with their fine
        instinct,
felt something beyond reverence.
                        In fact, at ceremonies,
with a show of great respect, they would touch the Herms' lips or
        phallus
(always sculpted erect), thereby drawing strength
for the days when, inevitably, the festival ends.

June 15, 1969

85 / Expiation

That boundary stone she hurled at Ares, struck his neck,
Loosed his limbs and down he crashed and out over seven acres
Spread the enormous god and his mane dragged in the dust,
His armor clashed around him . . .

ILIAD, XXI, 406–8
(translated by Robert Fagles)

The Greeks had little love for wild Ares. His
temples and statues were sparse. Athena always came out
the victor in battles between the two of them. His hair filled with
    dirt
as he fell to cover seven acres with his body. The artisans
accepted him only in naked form; they denied him his helmet;
his spear off to one side, abandoned on a chair, diagonally placed,
no longer a symbol—more a bit of decoration.
                                In that posture
we saw him one night when the moon was full, on the pediment
    of the Parthenon,
beautiful, mild-mannered—we admired him. We even gave him
    recognition
for good memories of our return from Troy, valuable experiences
and our joy in getting through so many dangers (of course the few
    of us
who survived. But as for the others? Who knows?)
                                      Later
we again depicted him nude, a daydreaming young man gazing
into the distance, passion playing between his strong legs.

Would that we could get along this time the way we did then. But
    now,
coming to our end, we won't give a damn about Ares
dressed or undressed—even though we'd already begun,
in the midst of the gunfire and the smoke, to make productive
    use of our new experiences,
secretly scratching on marble old known allegories
(his spear no longer at an angle now—better horizontal; and
    perched up there,
a bird: a sparrow or thrush or even that pigeon, the common
    variety).

June 19, 1969

The gods are being forgotten. And if we happened to remember
    Poseidon tonight
as we returned to the desolate shores of Kalavria,
it's because over here, in the sacred grove one July evening,
while oars gleamed in the moonlight and one could hear
the guitars of ivy-crowned young men in the rowboats,
here, in this pine-covered spot, Demosthenes took poison—
he, a stammerer, who struggled until he became the best orator of
    the Greeks,
and then, condemned by the Macedonians and the Athenians,
    learned, in the course of one night,
the most difficult, the greatest art of all: to be silent.

June 26, 1969

FROM

Railing

[1968-1969]

Difficult times, difficult in our country. And that proud one,
naked, unprotected, vulnerable, allowed them to help him.
They took out a mortgage on him, withheld fees. They make
    claims,
speak on his behalf, regulate his breathing, his pace.
They show compassion, dress him from head to toe in other
    clothes, loose-fitting,
they tie a hawser around his middle for a belt. He,
in alien clothes, doesn't speak or even smile any longer
for fear he'll show that between his teeth he holds—right up to
    sleep time,
very tightly, as though his ultimate contribution (only now
    actually his),
naked, gleaming and unyielding—his death.

November 7, 1968

He had to appear, it said, as soon as possible—that was written on
    the summons.
Where? When? In front of whom? For what kind of interrogation?
    As soon as possible, it said.
He turned it over. Nothing. He looked at it again. He hid it
under his mattress. Took it out again. Buried it in the closet.
Later he hid it in a crack in the floor. At noon
he closed the shutters, locked the door, went into the bedroom,
glanced secretly into the mirror, behind the curtain,
took out the piece of paper, went into the bathroom, tore it into
    little pieces,
threw it into the toilet. As he put out his hand to pull the chain,
the first helmeted man gripped his fingers, the other two held him
    by the shoulders.

February 1, 1969

93 / Readiness

I don't let this shadow fill up the house.
I light the chandeliers, I light the oil lamps.
I have matches available in every room, lanterns,
old and new candles. Two candlesticks
on either side of the stairs. I bang my cane against the wall—
this is my cane, I say, and this the wall. I ascertain,
classify, name. I prepare answers, pin
receipts to a wire. Above all,
at the four corners of the bed I ready—there they are—
the four standing candles and a white ribbon to bind the hands.

February 3, 1969

Evening clouds, the cathedral clock lit up,
disheveled trees, cold, trash. You could still hear
shooting up in the hills. A little later
George arrived on a bicycle. He set down a guitar
that had broken strings. "We've carried the dead bodies," he said,
"down to the warehouse. No anthems or flags.
Hide this list at least, so that tomorrow we remember
their names, their ages—I've even noted the size of their feet.
The three marble cutters were killed too. The only thing left
is that marble angel, headless—you can put any head you want on
    it."
That's what he said, then went off. He didn't take the guitar.

February 4, 1969

Newspapers: titles, titles, deaths, births, wars, deaths, marriages—
the same ones we read about last year. The bag over there with the
surgical instruments;
a long marble table; the other one, green: billiard table.
The good-looking boy with the tray listens behind the door.
Anatomy: didactic, tiring. The invariable. And anger all hollow.
Late at night a perforated moon comes up. The clouds run over
the hills.
Old chimney sweeps sit on the public park benches,
quiet old men, with bronchitis, retired now. "A black hole," they
say,
"the world is a black hole." They're quiet. They cough. They
don't get angry.
Analysis of soot, dissolution, blackness reconstituted. Across the
street,
behind the curtains, the light comes on. A little girl is playing the
piano.

February 5, 1969

Friday, Monday, Sunday, Wednesday, Saturday again—
we forget the order of days. Doors, windows, the color
violet, orange, purple, cypress trees, a flag with a hole in it,
a cigarette, two cigarettes, the mountain. Clouds went by. At
    twilight
the street lamps lit up early. The girls looked at their fractured
    faces
on the asphalt. It was drizzling. The bodies of the dead
were moved secretly at night. Since yesterday
they've been renovating the dairy shop. Behind the large window
the three helpers can be seen scrubbing the floor. The tables are
    getting wet out on the sidewalk.
In his ash-colored loft Petros used to make speeches in the old days.
He always talked about victories. He was certain. He hasn't been
    seen since.
Poetry remains closed from top to bottom. The air is not being
    renewed.

February 5, 1969

The first month they banned transportation and entertainment.
No ship appeared.
The closed circus of course suffered more than any of us. One day
the two small clowns came out with their clothes even looser than
usual, covered with rombuses,
multicolored rombuses, powdered noses, tears painted on.
They performed in the middle of the street, collected pennies in
their tambourine.
But nobody laughed. Then they wept in earnest,
made their painted tears run, smudged their faces.
One evening
they were apprehended, their hands were bound, they were taken
off to the large building.
The next day
when we woke, it was cloudy; the tents were gone from the square,
and the cages, the wagons.
A boy found a wet false beard under a tree, that was all.
He put on the beard hesitantly. "I'll save it for Santa Claus," he
said.

February 6, 1969

I told the carpenters, told the builders, told the electricians,
I told the grocer's delivery boy: "Secure that shutter;
all night long, loose-jointed, it bangs in the wind,
won't let me sleep. The owner is away. The house is becoming a
    ruin.
Nobody has been in it for twelve years. Secure it. I'll pay for it."
"We don't have the right," they said. "We can't interfere," they
    said.
"The owner's away. It's a stranger's house." That was just what I
    was hoping for,
what I wanted them to say, to recognize they had no right.
Let the shutter alone, let it bang in the wind over the garden,
over the empty cisterns with the slugs and the lizards,
with the scorpions, the empty spools, the broken glass. That noise
gives me an argument, allows me to sleep nights.

February 10, 1969

In time, houses collapse, the doors fade. In the garden
a rusted stove comes apart, crumbles, falls
like the leaves of a quince tree. In the afternoon it rains. The
    potholes
in the road fill up with water. Three old street lamps
light up beside the soccer field. The evening star
hovers over the mountain, very high up. A blue glow
comes out of the grocery-store doorway. The bicycle's shadow
grows longer on the wet road. With that shadow, that
minimal light, you might accomplish something deeper inside.
But poets are glorified for their worst poems.

February 11, 1969

They divided them into two teams, these on one side, those on the
    other.
They left no one in the middle. They took the clothes off their
    backs,
gave them uniforms—none fit properly. The groups began—
separately, of course—to exchange clothes. In the confusion
of this sorting out, along with that undefined fear of foreign,
unknown and inappropriate clothing, they suddenly heard
a great pealing of bells in the town. The governor had been
    murdered. The guards
had taken off. The doors all locked, the elevator stopped.
They, naked, waved their pants out of the window at those
who went by in the street below carrying flags. Then they tied
    their belts into a rope
and, naked that way, slid down into the courtyard, which was also
    locked.

February 18, 1969

He said: I believe in poetry, love, death—
that's precisely why I believe in immortality. I write a line of verse,
I write the world. I exist, the world exists.
A river flows from the tip of my little finger.
The sky is seven times blue. This clarity
is the primordial truth, my last will.

March 31, 1969

He said all difficult words so simply, so politely,
that it became clear he was disparaging us. Sometimes
he would resort to paradox, like a golden spot
on a white bird's left wing. We became embittered,
sometimes even enraged. Then he would take hold of our hands,
look deeply into our eyes like someone not responsible, or rather,
    like an accomplice.
After that he turned his back and pressed his forehead against the
    wall
as though pressing against the pane of a large window, gazing
at some unobstructed, floodlit landscape that we too had probably
    seen.

April 1, 1969

A small fisherman's house by the road. A flowery cotton curtain
in the window. They'd put the geranium pots
outside, against the wall. Through the half-opened door
you could see the chairs, the table, the lamp, the washbasin,
an embroidered Christ on the Cross, the baskets, the jug, the
    double bed,
multicolored rag rugs. On the sofa, the fat woman—
heavy, sweating, immobile, eyes closed—
was winding a ball, a large black wool ball,
her motion blind, ancient, independent. And outside
there was the sea, the golden sunset, swallows.

May 15, 1969

Broken vine-shoots, stones, thorns, a jug.
The patch of field is ruined. The house has been closed up for years.
Vangelis hasn't been back since then. Behind the stable
you can see a piece of the sea, dark blue. He'd sold
his horse during difficult times—a russet horse
with a white spot over its left eye. A seagull's down feather
fell on the dry twigs. The old woman in the doorway
across the street said: "With small things like that, my son,
we manage to make life livable." He didn't answer. He was looking
    into the distance.
He crossed himself and came forward as though to kiss
the old woman's hand or that down feather.

May 19, 1969

He takes up the clay, shapes the face, the body
beautiful, naked, serene—after what model?
those in the café, or in the temple, or among the demonstrators?
and that swarthy rower?
               The sun
comes through the door radiant, highlights
hollows and projections, creates body shadows
on the body.
           And the craftsman
blows his breath into the clay mouth—
a taste of earth stays on his lips.
Then he takes his hat, goes out into the street
with a guilty smile of secret happiness
as though playing the role of deaf-mute, which he really is.

May 30, 1969

Nobody had taken care of the garden for years. Still,
this year—in May, June—it flowered again by itself,
all on fire up to the fence: a thousand roses,
a thousand carnations, geraniums, a thousand sweet peas—
violet, orange, green, red and yellow,
colors, winged colors—to the point where the woman appeared
    again
to water with her old watering can: once again beautiful,
serene, with a certain assurance. And the garden
engulfed her up to the shoulders, embraced her, won her
    completely.
It raised her in its arms. And then we saw, in broad daylight,
that the garden and the woman with the watering can ascended,
and as we gazed on high, some drops from that watering can
fell softly on our cheeks, chin, lips.

June 3, 1969
Karlovasi, Samos

FROM

Doorman's Desk

$[1971]$

For years he was anxiously impatient. He would undress
in front of small or large mirrors,
in front of any windowpane; attentively
he would try out this or that stance in order to choose, to invent
the one most his, the one most natural, so that
his finished statue could be made—though he knew
that normally statues were fashioned
for the dead, or even more normally,
for certain unknown, nonexistent gods.

Athens, March 17, 1971

The man had gone to work long since. The woman
went into the bedroom, opened the drawer, took out
the bills for water, electricity, phone,
turned her back on the balcony door. "Let them
cut it all off," she said, "everything," as though she didn't know
they'd already cut everything off.
                              A swollen sun
flooded the large bed. A shadow evaporated
on the wall opposite. A fly sat on the washbasin
beside the ash tray, the alarm clock, the dead child's
blue ribbon. The two light-rich sheets
took on the shape of two blind statues lying down
for some half-hearted morning intercourse.
                              "Everything,
         everything," she said again.
And inside that "everything"—she could hear it—she found herself
speechless, calm, standing up straight, liberated, at one
with all things annihilated, killed, and surviving.

Athens, March 19, 1971

They set the café tables out on the sidewalk.
The old men come to sit there in the afternoon. The sunshine
stretches over their newspapers, wipes away the news.
They can't read any longer. Maybe they're angry about it too,
maybe they even forget, because death always
takes over the back pages of the newspaper
as it does the courtyards with the closed wells.
And it's quiet of an afternoon in the old neighborhood
as though all the pregnant women have moved to a new place.

Athens, March 20, 1971

Glory too is a road, he says:
the break in the road, along with the bridge,
there where you set down the basket with bread in it,
the knife, the napkin, on the low wall,
in an open place. And you, hidden,
behind the wall, towards sunset,
waiting for the first passerby to dine,
so you can see his teeth, his appetite,
hear the crumbs fall into the abyss
as he brushes the back of his hand
across his lips (or your lips) without
unfolding the white napkin.

Athens, March 25, 1971

113 / Correspondence

(a poet talks to a future poet)

If I didn't know that you would hear me one day
I wouldn't have anything more to offer, I wouldn't be able to speak,
and the spider who taught us the vertical ascent
on the blank wall would halt in my mouth,
forcing, straight into my throat,
the three black buttons of my jacket
and those other white buttons from the shirts of the dead.

Athens, March 28, 1971

He nailed the nail on the wall. He had nothing
to hang there. He gazed at it
from the old chair opposite. He couldn't
think of a thing, remember a thing. He got up,
covered the nail with his handkerchief. Suddenly
he saw his hand blackened, painted
by the moon standing in the window. The murderer
had lain down in his bed. His feet—
bare, strong, the toenails impeccable, a corn
on the little toe—extended well beyond the blanket,
and the hairs there curled erotically. The statues
always sleep that way: with eyes wide open,
and there's no reason to be afraid of any dream, any talk;
the faithful witness you needed, you now have—
the precisely spoken and discreet. Because, as you know,
the statues never betray, they only discover.

Athens, March 30, 1971

Now that you have nothing to say, nothing
to show, to propose, to defend—now
that everything is lost (and not only for you), precisely now
you're able to talk, circulating
among the implements of torture, turning
with your little finger the ridiculous wheels
of the ruined clocks or that big
hanging nonresistant wheel, still somehow damp
as it was when they brought it up from the sunken ship—

precisely now, drawing on the ropes attached to the ceiling,
hearing the noise of the pulleys above you
at certain indefinite points, like those stars that night
when we came back from the country, and in the marble forecourt
they'd set up in strict order
two rows of tall black wooden chairs
and in the middle the closed gold coffin of the king
without flags, without the crown and the sword.

Athens, April 1, 1971

To simplify things, to prefer
clean surfaces, the color white, the quiet
finished lines of the statues,
to continue his correspondence (he'd provided himself
with enough paper and envelopes the previous evening),
forgetting that small turtle, one foot
tied with string, hanging from the tree trunk,
the turtle he didn't dare set free, even though
there was no one there to see him.

Athens, April 3, 1971

There was nothing else in the night, just
the boundless dark plain and the straight road
almost invisibly lit from inside itself. Over there,
a huge smashed bus
with one headlight on, lighting up
the five wide-awake, startled chickens
and a dead branch of inviolability.

Athens, April 6, 1971

Late at night, when traffic thins out in the streets
and the traffic policemen give up their stations, he
doesn't know what to do any longer. He looks out
at the front window of the café opposite, steamed over
by the breath of insomnia; he looks at the waiters—
ghostly, refracted—changing clothes behind the cashier's desk;
he looks at the sky with its broad white cavities through which
you can see the wheels of the last bus. And then
this "nothing else, nothing else." He goes inside
the naked room, rests his forehead
on the shoulder of his own statue (larger than life),
feeling the morning's coolness in the marble, while below,
in the front courtyard with the broken flagstones, the guards
gather up the cut string from the exiles' bundles.

Athens, April 8, 1971

Say it, confess that certain thing,
that which you don't have to say—say it,
that which you don't know, that which doesn't exist,
calmly spreading the legs of the hanged man
as you would open the shutters at dawn
and put out your head to look down
at the empty street with its lamps still lit,
while the hunchbacked billposter glues
a huge yellow poster to the pillar upside down.

Athens, April 10, 1971

The wooden horse, the wooden queen, the wooden castle, the trees
on white and black tiles, carved with precision.
The discipline of the wooden soldiers. Diminished initiatives.
The chessboard left out on the roof terrace. Dampness. Moon
of a feigned spring, and the ancient owl. The hands,
in opposition and equally matched, meteors in the air, invisible,
    joined
in the compulsory handshake of a split, nonexistent victory
over the void, the measured "so-called." The two players
maybe went to the bathroom. There's the sound of water. The
    servant
comes out with the huge candlestick, sets it down on the table,
sits in the deep armchair, takes off one of his shoes,
closes his eyes, listens to the moths near the flame,
the slippery worms under the earth, between the roots,
opens his eyes, gazes at the candle, takes off his other shoe.

Athens, April 14, 1971

The three messengers arrived. They climbed the stairs.
The heralds left by the back door. A dog
went by tight against the wall. The odor of lilacs
entered the room of the man who'd been killed. The soldiers,
    outside,
took off their swords and helmets. They put them down
on the stones, hot from the sun.
                            Had the murderer
crossed the river? Had he made it out? And was it
he? Because doubles have multiplied lately.
A matter of habit, duplicate orders, the epidemic—
when someone looked at others, he had the impression
he was looking at himself in many mirrors. This
mitigated things somehow—a general guilt or pardon
and sometimes a general indifference.
                        But now,
nobody wanted to assume that kind of responsibility,
and one by one they began to stop resembling each other.
                                In the

    afternoon
we all joined the funeral procession. Then, opposite,
in front of the gate, between the two tall columns,
you could see the murderer standing up straight, reverently holding
the largest wreath made of white and red lilies.

Athens, April 16, 1971

Our mothers would die early. How did we grow up like this
in the hands of strangers? Winter mornings,
with a piece of wet bread and a little sugar. The alarm clocks
cut our sleep in half. We would go out into the street unwashed.
We would change houses every now and then, always leaving
     something behind:
a trunk with a few books, a broken mandolin.
We would go back some Sunday, we said, to pick them up.
We never went back. And that cloth suitcase
in the middle of the empty room, tattered,
with its belt bindings spread out on the floor—in that
we'd left an old talisman with black string,
along with those lewd photographs thumbed through a thousand
     times,
all of naked old-fashioned women with the broad pelvis,
small waist, and enormous breasts.
                    One of them
was lying face down as though crying. And she actually was crying
in front of the wall with the rusted nails
that were holding spread scissors and a pair of braces.

Athens, April 21, 1971

A bee settled on the windowpane. Then the sudden recollection
that this was Sunday, with the deep, closed stillness
of a white kitchen after the dishes are done.
And the dead sit speechless in the back rooms
in their old slippers, without making the slightest demand,
maybe just bothered a little by the absence
of any concrete interest and by the noise,
beyond the shutters, from the morning's first cicadas.

Athens, April 25, 1971

Maybe the houses will grow bigger. In contrast, people
constantly grow smaller. In the elevator
the three naked women, laughing, take up
a portrait of some bearded old man,
and in the elevator mirror, crowded in, shine
two broad hindquarters and the breasts of the third
and the dim back of the picture frame with the tiny spiders
and the dragging triangular fly-spat string.

Athens, May 19, 1971

It's a miracle, he says, more than a miracle:
there where everything is used up (I first of all) what do I find
among the pebbles at the sea's edge but the sacred skull
of one of Achilles' horses—maybe that of Xanthus. In the camomile
I find the Patriarch's staff.
I take it up devoutly, I climb the marble stairs,
I don't tap it on the steps, the crowd gathers,
I stand before the pulpit, I hear my hair become motionless,
loose on my shoulders. The crowd becomes impatient, people
     jostle each other;
I open my mouth to speak, and suddenly I realize
that I'm mute and that they hear me.

Athens, May 10, 1971

FROM

Sidestreet

$[1971\text{-}1972]$

He walks in the rain. He's in no hurry at all.
The wet railings glisten. The trees
are black, with a secret redness. A wheel
from an old bus lies abandoned in the sheepfold.
The blue house is infinitely more blue.
So this is how nothingness lightens. The stones fall.
Hands close. A blank file folder
comes down the river. But maybe
your name appears on the other side of it.

Samos, December 21, 1971

Down on the plain we saw the dead who had come down from the
     olive grove.
One wore a checked jacket, another carried a black umbrella.
The three of them were walking separately as though each had a
     more luxurious death.
The woman came well behind, limping, wearing a gray hat.
She had something in her pocketbook that she clinked—maybe
     glass beads.
We hid behind the sheepfold, afraid their shadow might fall on us.
From there you could see the snow-covered mountain gleaming
     in the sunshine.
Farther down, the prison tower with the bare flagpole.
If I were blind, Petros said—no, it wouldn't be better.
And as though to answer him, George said: see the blue groove
     in the snow?

Samos, December 23, 1971

We came back from the quay with an outdated ticket in our
    pockets,
with an old briefcase under our arms. Our suitcases
had been stolen from the hotel elevator. In the closet
the wire coat hangers remained empty—not quite empty:
still hanging there was a foreign pair of pants, broad, deep red,
with yellow rhombuses and green suspenders. The sea
could be seen from the window, and a thin line of cunning lights
far out on the horizon (maybe belonging to the ship that had left
    us behind).
In the bathroom where the foreign woman was washing her hair
you could hear the water soft with soap suds. And luckily people
were yelling so loudly below that the police with their dogs
couldn't possibly discover that we were stolen property.

Samos, December 25, 1971

When you go back home at night not knowing
why you went out, the front door-handle gleams
wet from the ancient metaphysical dampness
of the trees or the stars. You don't dare touch it.
The sound the key makes doesn't calm a thing. Then,
when you turn on the hallway light, everything
stays tightly locked up, stamped "FRAGILE,"
tied up with rope and string. "Vangeli," you shout,
"Vangeli, Vangeli." You wait. Your voice
goes out the chimney, comes back, climbs the stairs.
Nobody is sleeping in the second unmade bed.

Samos, December 25, 1971

The blind man is standing at the station. Women with cardboard
    boxes
get off the train. Under the single tree
they've left the hoe and the shovel. I don't know what it is, he says,
that makes the houses, the clouds, the streets change this way. I
    don't know
if I'm here or somewhere else. Noon moves on. From yellow
it turns to ashen. On the door of the small restaurant
you can see the print of an open palm—red,
maybe from red ink or blood. My Lord, he said,
it isn't my hand. And he showed his hands,
washed, clean, with a hole in the middle of the palm. And right
    away
he hid his face behind his hands so as not to reveal
the guilt, the remorse he felt because the blood wasn't his too.

Athens, December 27, 1971

In that space houses were built. You can't see
the bridge with passing bicycles. A woman
shakes out the sheets. The shadow grows oblique on the wall.
It was the hunger then, he says—the widened nostrils
outside the morning restaurants. The previous month
you would hear the blind men's guitar. Later,
neither the odor nor the guitar. Only the blind men
standing at the four corners of the street, not sad at all,
looking you in the eyes, ready to ask you
exactly what you were getting ready to ask,
and then, with double-edged voices, hawking lottery tickets
washed out by the sun, outdated by a year.

Athens, December 31, 1971

He was about to knock on the door. He changed his mind. He
    stood there.
Should he leave? How? What if the door suddenly opened?
And what if he were seen from the upstairs window? Suppose they
    were to throw out
a glass of water or cigarette butts or rotten flowers
or his two-day-old letter all torn up? It got dark.
Nobody went in or out. No window opened.
The house abandoned. Not a single light on over the stairs. On
    the floor
he could now clearly make out the two rusted forks,
a pile of soda bottles and empty cartridges,
and beside these a yellow mask identical with his face.

Athens, January 3, 1972

The three-story house is opposite the graveyard.
The women have got used to it. When they spread the laundry
on the balcony railing or the roof-terrace clothesline,
they gaze amicably at the marble kores and even more so
at the naked marble horseman—the little toe
on his left foot is broken (they know it,
they've touched it secretly). Down in the basement
lives the potter. He sets his jugs out in the sun,
a whole array of them on the sidewalk. When it gets dark
he takes them in. In black on red
he outlines the shadow of stalks of wheat in the earth, the shadow
    of the woman
undressing calmly in front of the lit window,
the hand raising an apple or a hawk, the boy
hiding his penis with his broad palm. This way
the dead no longer have anything to complain about or hate.

Athens, April 1, 1972

It was ground covered with large yellow thorns.
When the wind passed over it, there was noise.
A free void, uninhabited. The scorpion's tooth hidden.
Around dusk the place gave off flames.
Broken syringes and iron sparkled. The spiders
crossed the space from one thorn to another.
Above the thorns were large vessels.
Below the thorns were beaten children,
hatless old men, sullen women
with many miscarriages, slashed eyebrows,
a wooden cross at the throat. The old beggar woman
with the hole in her basket said: Lord, they now take away
even what we don't have. The eggs are white pebbles,
the rusks bricks, and I no longer have any place to hide
my embittered snake punctured by the thorns.

Athens, January 9, 1972

He hid them under the floorboards, spread the rug,
put the table and chairs back in place. He sat down,
calm now. He lit a cigarette. When they entered,
they headed straight there. They dug up the things.
Who had spotted him, and from where? Suddenly
he saw the reflection of those things
painted on the ceiling
as though they were lighted up inside. They took them.
They tied his hands. They dragged him outside.
And he between them in the street like a thief—
no, not at all frightened, only wondering:
might that reflection have stayed on the ceiling
golden like that among the shadows? Because of course
those things can't be hidden any longer.

Athens, January 14, 1972

As for me, I have my daily wage, he said. Forget the others.
I took a nail out of the wall, looked through the hole,
glued the glass pane with flour-and-water paste, smoked a cigarette.
I took the garbage can down to the curb
along with the cardboard box full of orange peels.
I combed my hair carefully, shined my shoes with spit,
ran a wet towel under my armpits,
stood at the window thinking. I spoke inside myself.
I'm ready now, ready at any moment—he says—
to present myself to the florist, the surgeon, or the prosecutor.

Athens, January 20, 1972

They moved to a new place every now and then. They'd take
a few suitcases with them, the essentials: handkerchiefs, socks,
very few souvenirs—the usual terms and names
for tools, plants, and birds. Maybe this gave them
a sense of familiarity with, of long-range mastery over,
that which they called "sometime" or "distant" or "never"
when drops of rain slid down their spines under their collars
and stopped at the small of the back, there where the shirt was
    held tight
by a leather belt. Because in that territory
it rains ceaselessly; invisible, hypertrophic plants grow
inside closed wells, where once they thoughtlessly threw in
graters, basins, cases, broken mirrors
and those small hydrocephalic unborn bodies.

Athens, January 28, 1972

This woman had a number of beautiful lovers. Now
she's bored; she doesn't dye her hair any more; she doesn't
remove the hairs with tweezers one by one around her mouth.
she stays in the wide bed until twelve noon.
She keeps her false teeth under the pillow. The men
circulate naked between one room and another. They often
go into the bathroom, close the faucets carefully,
by chance set a flower straight on the center table
as they pass through, noiseless, hideous, no stress now,
no impatience or impudence—the stress anyway
most easily discerned in its dying. Their heavy body hair
thins out, withers, turns white. The recumbent woman
closes her eyes so as not to see her toes
full of corns, disfigured—this once lusty woman.
She doesn't even have the strength to shut her eyes as much as
    she'd like,
obese, sunk in her fat, slack,
like poetry a few years after the revolution.

Athens, January 29, 1972

Maybe he buttoned his jacket askew on purpose.
One side hung low, the lapel opposite rose.
Every now and then he would scratch his chin—usually unshaven.
He told lies constantly, indifferent lies.
Nobody believed him; he didn't want to be believed.
Maybe given the general mistrust, he felt free.
When it rained he would sit in front of the window holding
scissors and a small mirror. He would trim his moustache
rhythmically, as though strictly timed (in fact
the metronome was working at 6/8 on the closed piano), like that,
as though carefully cutting raindrops one by one.

Athens, February 5, 1972

143 / Aids

I can't complain, he says. Yes, I know
the demolished houses. I know
the others due to be demolished, those
with the two clay caryatids standing
on either side of the entrance. Last evening
I saw the old man walking alone,
rapping the osiers with his staff,
his motion so young and beautiful,
as though all others were gone from the world.

Athens, February 15, 1972

There were still—beyond denial—certain places and events:
the gardener's footsteps beside the wall, the morning train
in the deserted station under fog, a dried-up lemon tree,
when they left the large wooden boxes on the stairs,
and the faces of the young were so distant, unreconciled, lovely,
changing the future almost into the present, approaching the
    windowpanes,
holding an apple in two fingers only, not knowing
whether to bite into it or to use it to break the mirror—
and later a certain word, every now and then, late at night, the
    moon out,
the word that is most ours, summer, between two strokes with the
    oars.

Athens, February 28, 1972

FROM

Muted Poems

$\left[\mathit{1972}\right]$

We saw the island's capers in the beggar's sack,
the old unmarried women behind the shutters,
from the window we saw the night melt away in the dawn.
The smells from the kitchens merged in the back stairwell.
The face of one woman was eaten away. Another
wore a yellow mask. In her apron pocket
she kept a small mirror and a watch. A sad-faced mouse
crossed under the staircase railing. In his teeth he held
the dead woman's chocolate bar. The third woman
gazed at the courtyard with its dried artichokes
and curled her fingers as though she'd been punctured. Everything
   —she said—
everything is a kind of penitence, without anyone having sinned.
The concierge appeared in the corridor with a tray
bearing the bull's head adorned all over with red ribbons.

Athens, March 23, 1972

Among the tourists, bus conductors,
small-time salesmen, photographers, cars,
the statues beside the oleanders gaze in our direction,
gaze at the particular spot that we covered
with tobacco leaves and newspapers. The statues,
their naked bodies shaded from the sun,
look in front of them quietly, purely, not at all accusingly,
so that we too turn and distinguish both them and ourselves.
Meanwhile the foreigners have left their baskets on the ground
full of little black crosses, yellow beads and belts.

Delphi, March 26, 1972

Endless transfers, unwanted or willed.
And suddenly time delays, holds back;
the dead disappear; those present: absent.
The table is set. Nothing's wrong. Come in.
The twelve glasses. And one more. Still, be careful,
don't step on the floor—there is no floor. Here
those who can sit comfortably are only those
who have eaten both of their wings and are no longer hungry.

Delphi, March 26, 1972

The old man is sitting on the chair, the old woman at the window.
From her stooped shoulder you gather that outside in the courtyard
there's a tree, possibly in blossom. Beyond the door
the inner part of the house stands mistrustfully with its vases,
its lost cutlery, its old photographs,
with a large curtain lying on the floor—the one
they planned to sew last summer
to diminish the light and the disharmony of the furniture.
But when the light lessened on its own, it wasn't necessary
to finish it, to add the rings, to hang it.
The thing stayed there, dead, in its long veil,
under the wooden stairway, turned toward the wall.

Athens, March 27, 1972

What more could he do, circulating day and night
among the ten blind men? He tried
invisible postures, indecipherable gestures—sometimes
completely naked, sometimes wearing the shirt and sword
of vanquished heroes, sometimes wearing the transparent dress
of the dead mythical woman; and the changes
always convincing, without need of proof. The blind men
ate a lot, slept well. In the evening
they chewed on their nails, listening to the radio
in the bar opposite. One of them washed his feet
in the metal basin. The second wore
a harlequin cap. The ninth—calm, standing—
contemplated the wall very close up. And he himself,
he knew perfectly well that the blind were not blind at all.

Athens, March 30, 1972

He who walks motionless through time with his hat
lowered to his eyes, with a piece of ice in his mouth—you
    recognize him
by his right hand always hidden in his pocket
(as though made of wood, covered by a brand-new coffee-colored
    glove)
clutching his identity card which he never wanted to show,
though maybe what's there is only the nail that held the seascape
with the empty red floating lifesavers and the huge lemons.

Athens, May 1, 1972

The smokestack, the church, the road, the taverna—all familiar.
In the dark room a fish circulates in the glass bowl.
He, alone, as always, observes—heedlessly—
the barely perceptible, moving gleam of the fish; and that sense
out of the absence of sensation. The slightest numbness
in his toes—the untried lethargy:
should he change position, light the lamp, or stay down there
in the paralytic's hypothetical wheelchair, from which he extends
his left hand to touch the iron rim of one wheel
as though holding on to the helm of an ancient, distant power,
tired and indifferent, not out to command anyone?
That's the way you hold on to the poem, like a secret you have
    sworn to keep
out of fear that it too no longer has anything to reveal.

Athens, May 9, 1972

They remain motionless, almost sad. They can't get angry any
    longer,
can't feel sorry for the others any longer. They remember a small
    balcony
that the acacias held high in their hands. They remember the
    aquarium
in a foreign city. A theatrical company had returned. The actors—
exhausted, failed—sat on their suitcases under the trees.
Their stage sets and wardrobes had been confiscated. Now
what costumes are they to play in, without red stage curtains and
    cardboard forests,
without the lions' gate, when even under the words
they'd memorized, or under their own, they've seen and recognized
    that same shade
for those who played the role of death so successfully, and for the
    others
who just as successfully played the role of deathlessness? On the
    grass below
lies a wooden knife wrapped in silver foil from chocolate bars.

Athens, May 10, 1972

Who bared the windows like that, the doors, the trees, the stones?
They stay back out of the way, discreet, pretending not to see.
They actually don't see. They let the hanged man free to swing
    on his rope,
the soldier to piss in the sheepfold, the woman with her single
    earring,
the crone with her basket of eggs. The florist sprinkles the red lilies;
if they were made out of paper they'd surely disintegrate— but in
    fact they're not. Here I am—he says—
left alone with these continual subtractions (and they don't even
    ask me)
alone, yes, countersigning them quietly, in capitals and in beautiful
    script.

Athens, May 11, 1972

Close the windows tightly. Draw the curtains.
The darkness is green under the trees. The sick women
sit on the benches with the masks of the blind men.
Their hair turns heavy from the dampness. Don't look at them.
Don't ask them anything. They don't answer. On their knees they
    hold
the jester's red cap—they found it one night
on the soccer field under the moon. And it's the same one
you had decorated with a row of small bells
announcing familiar, diverting festivals—don't deny it; I know.
Now they've taken out the small metal tongue from those bells
and they hold them in their mouths—maybe tasting them; that's
    why they don't talk.
You see, the time comes when lying is no longer tolerable
even to that handsome, polite, that most innocent liar in the world,
the one with the wide sleeves for hiding his bound hands.

Athens, May 19, 1972

Things seen (certainly these, and by these, he says), looked at
through the fixed wooden eyes of the giant crab, at night,
when the river cuts through the house along with the stars,
the cigarette butts, the squeezed lemons, the eggshells. Every now
    and then
a dry branch hooks itself on a chair leg;
the motion stops suddenly the way a mouth opens. And he
who always confesses his unhappiness easily now finds himself
without any death at all, without any justification. He bends,
picks up that branch, sets it down on the table; his hands are wet;
he wipes them secretly on his pants; and then he sees—
opposite him, on the huge couch—the three dead men with their
    high collars,
their tall, shining hats on their knees,
motionless, fixed, waiting to be photographed.

Athens, May 19, 1972

These comparisons always humiliate him: he jumps
from one thing to its opposite or stays more or less in the middle,
    a little below or a little above.
He doesn't forgive himself whatever the action or position; only
from wherever he returns he brings as booty, with hidden pride,
a bared kernel of rice on which he has patiently carved
a multitude of war scenes, heroes, dead men, trees, flags,
and that beautiful, crazy deserter who, naked in front of the gun
    barrels,
endlessly drums away on his empty canteen.

Athens, May 19, 1972

Since last year, he says, I've had a beautiful yellow shirt.
That's why I waited for summer this year—so I could wear it.
I always talk in a loud voice on the phone. I have the feeling
that I'm not being heard. Later, of course, I saw
that however loud or soft you talk, nobody listens.
I amuse myself by saying this is the age of the deaf and dumb.
    Anyway
my toes are beautiful like those of the statues—
it suits me to walk or stand on marble,
except that I feel the quiet cold on my soles, and sometimes
a thumbtack fallen from the architect's table
forces me to bend down in order to pick it up. This exactly
is the degrading difference between me and the statues.

Athens, May 22, 1972

I climbed up on the chair, he says, took the curtain down,
spread it on the bed, painted large red storks
all over it, hung it back in place again.
The house filled up with birds; but now they're blue.
I can't catch a single one. I call out to them, invent
lovely names for them so they'll listen to me, so they'll sit
on my knees or on the washbasin or the hanger.
They won't sit; they fly off. I close the shutters to lock them in.
No longer blue or red, only black, black, black.
They've fallen to the floor dead; I don't hear them, don't see them.
And I can't move, can't turn on the light, for fear of stepping on
    them.

Athens, June 1, 1972

Years, windows, blankets, a small black ship,
its upper deck lit up by the sunset. Four windowpanes
over dark green water. You can still make out
the naked drowned men wearing their wristwatches. The one
has his left eye open—it's a glass eye; it won't shut.
The women came down, covered them with sheets. Then
the customs officers showed up, sent the women away.
The cyclist brought an acetylene torch from the taverna.
He leaned his bicycle against the railing. And suddenly the quay
radiated yellow to the far end, clearly revealing the one
who was going off with the giant strides of an ancient runner—
the one who, in the confusion, had stolen the glass eye.

Athens, June 2, 1972

He usually likes to talk about things he doesn't know
or doesn't understand. He himself admits it. Still,
he knows the chimney opposite very well, black in the red sunset,
from where night descends on the furniture in the house. And he
    even knows
the feel of chalk—for years he's had a piece hidden away
in the bottom drawer of his desk. On the wall the photograph:
the three old women standing upright, arms linking them at the
    waist,
with long dark dresses. Two of them are smiling. The middle one
is tight-lipped (just two days earlier
her front teeth fell out). And it suits her,
this tight-lipped image, because in this way, the word—
that final word of condemnation, the irrevocable one—
hasn't been spoken. And all her bitterness is transformed little by
    little,
sweetening her very saliva with the victory of silence kept.
On the dress of this one in the middle, a bit above her black,
    laced-up shoes,
you see the imprint of the itinerant photographer's head.

Athens, June 3, 1972

What we didn't say became barbed wire again. The women
sat under the trees. They waited. Their hair
caught up fluff from thorns, flying ants, spiders,
tiny butterflies and leaves. When night fell, they were sent away.
They took back the napkins with bread and cigarettes in them,
the silence of the earth they sat on, the folded handkerchief
with the small shaving mirror inside it. When they reached home,
they hid the mirror under a pillow, moved
the huge trunk with a man's strength so their children wouldn't
    see
that they'd left the ash tray under the table,
along with the red stockings full of holes and the black scissors.

Kalamos, June 18, 1972

They sat on the well's lip. They looked down inside. The water
was deep, dark, with a few white stains.
What if a pipe fell out of somebody's pocket, a toothpick,
the key, a comb, or that secret photograph
of the generously endowed naked woman with the lilies on her
   breasts?
She had a bracelet on her left ankle. A nail hole
showed on her upper body—because, in those days,
he had her permanently nailed on the wall. And you could hear
an old grandfather clock ticking away right behind the photograph,
in the crone's room next door. "It's her heart," he said.
"Not the crone's," he explained, "maybe that's just a coincidence."
   And suddenly
the dark water rose and drowned them. The next day
we found, floating on the water with evident prosperity,
that same plump woman. She wasn't wearing a bracelet on her
   ankle.

Kalamos, June 18, 1972

165 / Wind

Sudden summer wind behind the shutters.
The women's dresses billowed out. Small warmed birds
left their armpits. The nannies take refuge
in the hallways, they roll up the rugs. A glass
assumes the role of prophet on a chair. From across the way
you can hear the hammers striking the raised planks. The tightrope
  walker
gazes out the window at the cut rope dangling from the two poles.
A huge piece of yellow cardboard limps across the terrace. Iron
  hoops
from the old cellar barrels roll in the streets. I
didn't know a thing, he says; they took me, I went along with them
  peacefully,
I stopped only for a moment, startled: there was no whitewash on
  the walls.
Great collapsed cauldrons stumbled against our knees.
I then told them candidly: the dead are no longer frightened.
I even showed them the mirror. Inside it, at an angle, you could see
the geologist with that hearing-aid wire of his secretly listening.

Athens, June 21, 1972

That which began as a wrestling match turned little by little
into a familiar, forgotten dance. The two antagonists,
beautiful, muscular, robust, with faces lit up,
moved from rivalry to consent. They ended
by embracing erotically in front of our eyes. And we,
wearing large, red, aroused masks,
gave them a standing ovation, cheered, wept,
throwing off our clothes piece by piece, having abandoned
our watches and our trowels on the seats.

Athens, June 22, 1972

The house closed up tight. Raging cicadas sounded outside the
    shutters.
The dog had died. The caretaker had left years ago.
The rope tied around the trunk of the mulberry tree: now in
    shreds.
Pine trees and olive trees laid waste by the scorching sun. The sea
    drowned
in its own salt. At noon the two aged women arrived.
They left their umbrellas, their hats, on the table.
Silently they undid the four packages; they went into the kitchen;
they set out poison for the mice, for the cockroaches.
They put away the paper and the string in their purses.
In the bathroom a huge May beetle was buzzing. They heard it.
    Then
they suddenly understood that everything was over. The two of
    them stood
in front of the dusty wardrobe mirror. Without ceremony
they changed their hats. They locked up and left—
dry, thin, unmoved by the old spring portraits of them
hanging in the locked house. And abruptly, there, in the middle of
    the road,
they both began to limp ostentatiously, favoring the right side.

Kalamos, June 25, 1972

A piece of red cloth against the dark blue.
Olive trees, poles, plastic bags, bathers kissing,
faces, hands, bodies spoiled by time;
bitterly, bitterly sustained interests. The crickets—
voices abandoned in space; you didn't notice them—foreign voices.
You hear them or you don't, see them or don't—nothing, nothing,
    he said.
A forgotten astringent odor from cut grass.
So sit down here on the ground, on the warmed earth.
Undo the knots in the napkin one by one, eat your bread,
biting deeply, farther in than death. And then,
with dusk, the eggshells—so white and fragile—
creaking under the feet of the great blind man heading calmly
toward the altar of Colonus, guided by a small tortoise.

Kalamos, June 25, 1972

FROM

Paper Poems

$[1973\text{-}1974]$

The washbasin in the yard.
We took soot
and drew old black women
on the white wall.
The bird came
and added red.

Then when you were in pain
when you were afraid
all the buttons on your jacket
cut off
half naked
more than naked
you couldn't see the eagles any longer
they were under your feet.

I sinned, he said.
I'm human.
How else?
I don't always have
the key
tucked in my belt.
Often I stay
outside my house
with sky only
and the bones of my dog.

Loquacious dreams
wasteful words.
My stingy moon
we two
alone
secretly at the corner
pissing.

The sparrows knew him
they sat on his knees
they pecked his fingers
they went into his pockets.
There
the little saint
his hair in barbed wire
grabbed them, choked them.

He said:
I will bring you wings
and a tray full of cakes.
Whatever you want.
Through the windowpane
I'll watch you
bind my wings to your breasts
with sugar-coated fingers.
I'll fly the wrong way round.

It was a glass house
empty
inside it
the emptiness showed
and the copper ring
on the ceiling.
In the basement
the rusted mouse trap
and a green boot
belonging to the forest guard.
I brought them the judge:
sole proof.

The poem
year after year
searches for its reader.
There
it falls on its knees
under the shadow
of the largest wings
in the deepest night
with the empty garden benches
with the hooks in the trees.

What do you want to say?
I forgot.
They interrupt me constantly
I always forget the main thing
maybe not by accident.
At dawn
I fall asleep in the chair.
I feel her little finger
drift across my eyelids
the most distant gratitude.
Maybe that's what I wanted to say.
The thing I forget.

He had nothing more to say.
He moved over to the mirror,
pressed his forehead
against his forehead
until nothing was left
except the five chairs—
on one, the white gloves,
on another, the saw.

Those who
defend us
simply
almost without knowing it
cutting a piece of grass
and chewing it,
hungry.
Don't forget them.

In place of the collapsed roof
the sky—
we couldn't see it.
The fallen roof
showed more clearly
and the blind dog
invisible
under the beam
barking.

The other things farther under the stone
farther below the water
deeper
could be postponed.
Now
the eye fixed on the point
of the deeper thing
of the water of the tree
of the root
that the dead
scratch with their nails.

You will dig again where you dug before
you will rebuild where you built before
you will carry the door on your shoulders
you will transport
the wounded the dead the newly born
on this door
without a key to fit it
without need for a key.
And the salt poured out on the slate paving.

You sealed the cracks in the windows
with cotton
the ears the eyes the nostrils
the mouth.
A lot of cotton.
Night after night you chewed on it
you spun it with your teeth
you brought out colored ribbons
tied them on the shutters
on the barbed wire
and on one table leg.

Picking his nose
scratching his balls
sowing teeth in the earth.
The facade collapsed
covering passersby
the itinerant florist
the bicycle rider
leaving intact the framed portraits
on the inner walls—
portraits of those executed.

That which you avoid.
This straw for the horses.
These branches for the fire.
They slaughtered the horses on the road.
They didn't light a fire.
With the straw
they filled the cloth dolls in the tailor shops
they filled the farmers' scarecrows
to scare the wolves
to scare the ravens
to scare you who made it
this grieving scarecrow.

He preferred the black and the red.
(The only ones there were).
He left them on the table.
He didn't paint.
He approached the mirror.
He painted his face.
Black only.
To hide the red.

Denial has the taste
of trod grass
of a cut wing
of pride.
Between the wolf's teeth
the prince's golden belt.
How long will the hunger last?
How long
will the donkey's hide last?

That story has ended too.
Nothing arrives on time.
Nothing ends on time.
The door closed.
The phone went dead.
Fortunately, he said,
I can forget to remember
to be
to economize again
to put the noble statuettes I made
in the refrigerator
kneading the morsels of bread
with spit in my mouth—
the bread I didn't eat.

The wings you wore were too heavy
they weighed you down
you didn't fly.
And how many
dead birds.

Peelings from flayed walls
in the hair on the shoulders
and worst of all in the pockets
when it begins to rain
in the poor grocery stores
in the dirty fishmongers'
and the huge eyes
of the dead fish
pretend not to see us.

Wipe your glasses
on the corner of the red curtain
so they don't realize
that defective vision
sees deeper.

Every gesture
(including the most absentminded—
that in particular)
covers the great delay.
Then they turn on the lights.
We eat forget chatter
separate.
That delay motionless
behind the long curtain.
(Is that where we met?)
And the napkin
unfolded, stepped on
under the table.

Mean old women with candles and sheets
in huge uninhabited rooms
framed portraits of ancestors in the hallway
with their broken glass
string tied to the nails
from one wall to the next.
The guard
threw his underpants on the table
his shoes at the moon
the mice climbed the stairs.
O cock cock of betrayal
my brother my twisted one my witness
one of your wings golden on my hat
the other black in my pocket.

Athens, January–June 1973

Invulnerable body all naked
so point-blank naked
with the nipples still erect
invulnerable
to interior or exterior gunfire
and that blue triumphant cunning
and the wide trowel in hand
covering with cement
the smile of the second Christ.

Hidden
behind the massive statue of Zeus
he waits for the lights to go out
the guards to leave.
The reflection from the Garden lights
is enough.
He knows each detail.
The marble is already warmed up.
The hand knows where it will move.

People drenched by the rain
doors closed lowered lights mud
hidden flags.
You've got to change your mind
look elsewhere
quiet down
until the jaws relax
so the silence doesn't creak.

The warriors returned at midnight
then the others, more and more of them.
Unshaven faces
wet boots
fear.
They all talked about battles
nobody about victories
they all turned silent
along with the dead.
And the knife nailed to the wall.

At night there's a lot of noise
in the corridor.
The guards come back. They undress.
They pull the nails out of their boots
nail the naked women on the wall.
Small rivers run along the cement.

Of course it's easy to receive the others.
But you yourself?
When you take a walk
gazing ahead of you,
your eyes
transferred to the back of your head
hidden in your hair
almost closed
gaze straight behind
at the same point.

You touched
the night's dampness
on the woman's skin.
A leaf falls.
The color changes.
Black drowned in red.
After that
the black blacker.

Under the stillness
lies the great blow.
Pretend you don't hear.
I won't tell either.
How many beautiful things
depicted on the fallen shield—
that didn't protect us either,
didn't hide us.
Now it's up to the pyre.

Who made
this exquisite statue
fallen from its pedestal
all muddy,
and its faithful dog
showing its teeth
not at all with rage
with contempt?

How demonstrate
what is necessary
what is great
under the whip
under the scornful laughter
of the dressed guards
while you're naked
your genitals
completely gone
out of fear
and opposite you the kite
caught in the tree
its six torn wings
flapping in the dusk.

He read the small advertisements
noted on his cigarette pack
names numbers addresses
words
he changed trades.
In the end he put on the large goggles of a welder
gazed at the night
felt a pain in his side.

I unmasked him, he said—the blind man.
I told him in front of the world:
don't pretend you can't see.
I took his hat off his knees
I took his coins
he got up
kissed me on the mouth
we wept together.
The kindhearted woman appeared
wiped our eyes
took us to her bed.

He brought the compass from the ship
left it on the table
took off his cap
took off his shoes
couldn't sleep.
Where are the four points of the horizon
where is the body's center
how far does the periphery extend
how is the final contradiction realized?

I can't stand it, he said.
What other road?
Season of the hungry dogs
season of forgetfulness and memory
season of disguises
season of swindlers
season of broken doors.
I gave a penny to the blind man
I climbed down from the stands stooped over
unbuttoned my pants
season of no raised flags.

That same night
a short time after the fire
the wooden horse
huge, empty
without the warriors in its guts
opened its jaws
without teeth
and spoke:
Is it the Trojans you deceived
or maybe yourselves?
The blood rolled all the way down to the shore.

Athens, Kalamos, June 1973–May 1974

"From *The Wall Inside the Mirror* (1967–1968, 1971)": As the dates in the parenthesis suggest, this volume offers related work from two different periods under the 1967–1974 dictatorship. The division occurs after the poem "Return."

"Transgression": The "wooden horse" is presumably an allusion to the Trojan Horse, offered here, one assumes, as an ironic comment on the Greek predicament under the dictatorship.

"Our Land": It is customary in the Greek Orthodox Church for those returning home with lighted candles from the Resurrection Service on Easter Eve to mark a cross with soot from these candles on the lintel above the entrance doorway to their homes. This is meant to carry forward the implications of the service through the year following and to bring good luck. Outside the context of Ritsos's poem, it is of course the living, not the dead, who inscribe the crosses and who are given new life by the resurrected Christ.

"Continued Waiting": The covert allusions in this poem to Christ, Judas, and the other disciples are typical of Ritsos's use of Christian sources to parallel his use of ancient Greek mythology during the period of the 1967–1974 dictatorship.

"Exploration": See the note to "Transgression" above.

"Change of Habits": "The place" in line 4 presumably refers to a staging area for forced departure into exile on one of the prison islands early during the 1967–1974 dictatorship.

"Return": The poet's footnote to this poem, and the dating of individual poems in the French translation of *The Wall Inside the Mirror* (trans. Dominique Grandmont, Gallimard, Paris, 1973), the first presentation of the poems, indicate that Ritsos wrote the November 1967–January 1968 portion of the volume while in political exile on the prison island of Leros. The Greek edition of 1974 (Kedros, Athens) does not offer a place and date of composition for individual poems except for this one and "The Jester's Secret," the poem that concludes the volume, where the poet's footnote reads "Athens, Samos / March–October

1971." From the footnotes in the French translation we can gather that the poems of the second portion of the volume were written not only in Athens and on Samos (where the poet spent some time under house arrest in the company of his wife, a practicing physician on the island) but also in the mainland towns of Corinth and Delphi.

"Sunday Excursion": "Petros" and "Yannis" are the Greek forms of Peter and John—Christian names as common in Greece as elsewhere.

"The Jester's Secret": The places and dates in the poet's footnote are discussed in the note on "Return" above.

"From *Stones* (1968)": The poet indicates in a note to this volume and the two following volumes (which appear with it in the Greek edition) that the dates given in footnotes to the poems in these three volumes "are those of the first draft and not of the final version that emerged from successive revisions at other times and in other places. This has always been the poet's practice, in his short poems, even if the changes were of a kind and number to preclude any recollection of the poem's initial design."

"Night": The date and place in the poet's footnote indicate that the first drafts of the poems in this volume (see the above note), along with the first portion of *The Wall Inside the Mirror*, were completed while the poet was still in exile on the prison island of Leros.

"The New Oracle": "The Pythia" refers to the medium of Apollo's oracle at Delphi. Trophonius was a Boeotian oracular god who was reputed to have built Apollo's temple at Delphi and subsequently to have given out oracles from a mountainside above the sacred grove at Lebadeia (now Levadia), his shrine there much revered by the ancient Greeks and a source of elaborate rituals (see Pausanias, IX. 39 ff.) Saon was the eldest of the ambassadors sent to discover the oracle by way of Delphi, and he did so by following a swarm of bees to a place where they flew into the earth, thereby signaling the oracle. He learned from Trophonius himself the liturgy and rites celebrated there.

"The Tomb of Our Ancestors": According to Herodotus (I. 67–68), during the mid sixth century B.C. the Pythian priestess at Delphi declared that in order for Sparta to come out victorious over Tegea after a continuing failure to do so, Sparta had to bring home the bones of Orestes, son of Agamemnon, from his place of burial in Tegea. The Spartan Lichas, hearing from a Tegean blacksmith about a corpse of unusual length (seven cubits) buried in his courtyard, managed, through the subterfuge of posing as a banished exile and after much persuasion, to gain access to the blacksmith's courtyard, where he found the bones of Orestes, dug them out, and carried them back to his home city. Thereafter, Sparta got the better of Tegea on the battlefield.

"After the Defeat": The last Athenian fleet in the Peloponnesian War was defeated and destroyed at Aegospotami in the Hellespont in 405 B.C. and Athens capitulated to Sparta in April, 414 B.C. The Thirty Tyrants who seized full power in Athens following the end of the Peloponnesian War promoted a reign of terror during which hundreds of citizens were executed and their property confiscated. "Kimon" alludes to the famous Athenian statesman and military leader who was influential during the first half of the fifth century B.C. Plutarch reports that when Kimon conquered the island of Skyros he searched for the bones of the demigod Theseus that were buried there in order to return them to Athens for honorable burial as the Delphic oracle had recommended. Kimon saw an eagle pecking at a mound and tearing up the earth with its talons. He dug there and found the coffin of a man of gigantic size, a bronze spear and a sword lying by his side. Kimon brought these relics back to Athens and was received with grand processions and sacrifices as though Theseus himself had returned to the city.

"Alcmene": Alcmene, married to Amphitryon, refused to sleep with her husband until he avenged the death of her brothers at the hands of the Teleboans. He gathered an army, and on the night of his victorious return from the mission, Alcmene was visited by Zeus disguised as

Amphitryon and, shortly after, by Amphitryon himself. As a conse-
quence of her union with the god, she bore Heracles, twin to
Amphitryon's son Iphicles.

"Philomela": Tereus was married to Procne, sister of Philomela. According
to one version of the legend, he was sent to collect Philomela, fell in
love with her during the journey home, then raped her, then cut out her
tongue to prevent her from revealing the deed, finally confined her to a
lonely castle. Philomela wove the story of her tribulations into a piece
of embroidery and sent it to Procne, who found her sister and then
punished her husband by killing their son Itys and serving Tereus the
child's flesh for dinner at a Bacchic festival in Daulis. Tereus drew
his sword and pursued the sisters, but as he was about to slay them,
the gods changed him into a hoopoe, Procne into a swallow, and
Philomela into a nightingale.

"The Decay of the Argo": The Argo, Jason's ship for the voyage to Colchis
with a crew of heroes to find the Golden Fleece, was the first longship
made, built by Argos with the help of the goddess Athena, who, accord-
ing to Apollodoros, took a plank from the sacred oak at Dodona (see
the note to "The End of Dodona I" below) and built it into the keel
so that the Argo could speak. Apollodoros also tells us that Jason, on
his successful return to Greece, sailed with his chiefs to the Isthmus of
Corinth to dedicate the Argo to Poseidon at the god's sanctuary there.

"Penelope's Despair": Homer's account of Odysseus's reunion with a less
despairing Penelope is given in Book XXIII of the *Odyssey*.

"The End of Dodona I": Dodona, in the mountains of Epirus, was home to
an ancient oracle of Zeus. The god's will was derived from the rustling
leaves of a sacred oak, from the cooing of sacred doves, from the echoes
produced by cauldron tripods, and, according to Servius's commentary
on Vergil, from the murmur of a fountain or spring flowing from the
roots of the large oak. One legend has it that the woodcutter Hellos
attempted to cut down the sacred oak but was warned against this
unwitting impiety by a dove perched on the tree; the woodcutter let his

axe fall to the ground (where it still lies, Philostratus tells us) and became the first of Zeus's priests at Dodona. Servius mentions that the sacred oak was ordered to be cut down (at an unspecified time) by Arkes, an Illyrian bandit. Among the surviving questions asked the oracle at Dodona, several have to do with whether or not the inquirer will have offspring, and one concerns whether "it is better and profitable for [Cleotas] to keep sheep" (see N. W. Parke, *The Oracles of Zeus*, Oxford, 1967, pp. 265 and 268).

"The End of Dodona II": Dione, consort of Zeus at Dodona, was presumed to be the mother of Aphrodite. Roman Emperor of the East during the late fourth century A.D., Theodosius I, "the Great," was a strict Athanasian who imposed orthodoxy throughout the territory he ruled, Dodona included, and overcame whatever lingering resistance to Christianity there was.

"The Lone Plow": The Areopagus, located on a hill known by that name to the northwest of the Athenian acropolis, was said to have been founded by Athena to serve as the seat of justice in Athens, especially for cases of homicide. The name still designates the highest court of appeal in the Greek judicial system. Of the three sacred plowings in the ancient Athenian festival year, the most sacred took place at the Bouzygion at the foot of the Acropolis. The plow was invented by the Athenian hero Bouzeges, and his plow was preserved on the Acropolis as a votive offering.

"Marpessa's Choice": Marpessa, daughter of Ares' son Euenus, was the bride of Idas, the "strongest of men then on earth," according to Homer (*Iliad*, 9. 558). Apollo tried to carry her off, but Idas followed the god with bow and arrows ready. The confrontation between god and mortal resolved when Zeus gave Marpessa her choice between the two and she chose her mortal husband because she feared Apollo would desert her when she got old.

"The Real Reason": Cassandra, the most beautiful of Priam and Hecuba's daughters, was loved by Apollo, who offered her whatever she might want in return for allowing him to gratify his passion. She asked for the gift of prophecy, but when it was granted her, she refused to honor her side of the bargain and slighted the god. In his disappointment, Apollo ordained that no one should believe her prophecies, however true. Agamemnon, who took her home with him as booty from Troy, was among these. Despite Cassandra's warnings of calamity ahead, Agamemnon returns from Troy to Mycenae to walk the purple carpet into his palace under the persuasion of his wife Clytemnestra and finds himself caught up in a net in his bath and murdered there by Clytemnestra and her lover Aegisthus. Though Cassandra foresees both Agamemnon's fate and her own, her lamenting is of no consequence, and she follows him into the palace to face her death at the hands of Clytemnestra.

"Apollo's First Altar": Legend has it that after Apollo slew the dragon called Python at Delphi, the god took the shape of a dolphin, hailed a Cretan merchant ship on its way from Knossos to Pylos, and turned it toward the shores of Phocis. When it ran aground near Chrissa (sometimes spelled 'Crisa' or 'Krisa'), he assumed the form of a radiant young man and led the ship's passengers and crew to his Delphic sanctuary, where they served as the first ministers of his cult.

"Herms II": Herms were pillars of marble or bronze that stood in various streets and squares of Athens and other Greek cities. The pillars were normally surmounted by a bust of the god Hermes, with projections near the shoulders to hold wreaths and, during the classical period, with genitals, the phallus erect. During the sixth century B.C. Hipparchus, son of Pisistratus, set up herm milestones in Attica giving the distances from Athens.

"Expiation": Ares, son of Zeus and Hera, was the god of war, or the wild spirit of war. He was in fact a relatively unpopular deity, important only in Thebes and Athens, represented in mythology either as the instigator of violent behavior or as a stormy, unchivalrous lover. Lines 5–10 refer to the seated Ares on the east frieze of the Parthenon. Lines

14–16 refer to the sculpture Ares Ludovisi.

"Requiem on Poros": Demosthenes (383–322 B.C.), generally regarded as the greatest of Greek orators, was said to have overcome his early imperfect delivery by rigorous training (he apparently had difficulty pronouncing the Greek "r" in particular). He became an important political leader in Athens, especially in opposition to the rise of Macedonia. After the death of Alexander the Great and the victory of the Macedonians at Crannon under Antipater, Demosthenes was ordered to be executed. He took sanctuary in the temple of Poseidon on the island of Calauria (Kalavria, Poros), but under pursuit there, he committed suicide by sucking poison concealed in the end of his pen.

"Readiness": In Greece the hands of the dead are sometimes bound by a ribbon.

"Greece": "Vangelis" is a common Greek diminutive of the Christian name "Evangelos."

"Renaissance": Karlovasi is the town on the island of Samos where Ritsos lived under house arrest during the 1967–1974 dictatorship and where he normally spends his summers.

"From *Doorman's Desk* (1971)": The doorman (supervisor) of an apartment building in Athens and elsewhere usually has a cubicle with a desk in it on one side of the front lobby.

"The Miracle": In mythology, the horses of Achilles, Balius and Xanthus, were immortal. The poem appears outside chronological order as in the Greek edition.

"Return": For "Vangeli," see the note to "Greece" above.

"Cohabitation": Kores are archaic sculptures of young unmarried women, once plentiful on the Athenian acropolis.

"Aids": Caryatids are draped female statues serving as columns or pilasters, as in the Erechtheum on the Athenian acropolis.

"Fellow Diners": See the note to "Continued Waiting" above.

"The Same Course": The allusion is presumably to blinded Oedipus at the end of his days.

"From *Paper Poems* (1973–1974)": The volume *Paper Poems* in the Greek edition includes three series of poems, two of which are represented here. Selections from the first series can be found in *Yannis Ritsos: Selected Poems*, translated by Nikos Stangos (Penguin, London, 1974; Athens 1983).

"That same night . . .": See the note to "Transgression" above.